SCIENTIFIC FRENCH

by **WILLIAM N. LOCKE**

Head of the Department of Modern Languages

Massachusetts Institute of Technology

SCIENTIFIC FRENCH

A CONCISE DESCRIPTION OF THE STRUCTURAL ELEMENTS

OF SCIENTIFIC AND TECHNICAL FRENCH

ROBERT E. KRIEGER PUBLISHING COMPANY
HUNTINGTON, NEW YORK
1979

Original Edition 1957
Reprint Edition 1979

Printed and Published by
ROBERT E. KRIEGER PUBLISHING COMPANY
645 NEW YORK AVENUE
HUNTINGTON, NEW YORK 11743

Copyright © 1957 by
JOHN WILEY & SONS, INC.
Reprinted by Arrangement

Printed in the United States of America

Library of Congress Cataloging in Publication Data

Locke, William Nash, 1909-
    Scientific French.

    Reprint of the ed. published by Wiley, New York.
    1. French language—Technical French.   I. Title.
[PC2120.S3L6   1979]   448'.2'421   78-11669
ISBN 0-88275-771-7

Preface

This book is intended to fill a need not ordinarily met by elementary language texts. The young scientist or engineer, as well as the student preparing for these professions, is frequently faced by the problem of acquiring rapidly and directly a reading knowledge of French adequate to cope with technical articles and books in his field. This book is designed to be used from the very beginning in conjunction with readings from unsimplified scientific and technical material and with a dictionary. It is meant primarily for beginners with no previous knowledge of French, but can also be used by those who wish to refresh their knowledge of the language. It can be used in classes or for individual study.

Two types of difficulty face the student trying to read a foreign language. The first arises from the simple and obvious fact that the same object or concept is described by a different word in a different language, with the complicating factor that the area of meaning covered by one word in language A may be subdivided among two or three words in language B. The learner at first tends to think of his difficulties in these terms. And, in fact, they can be resolved with relative ease, given a certain amount of language sense, by consulting a dictionary.

There are other difficulties for which the dictionary offers no solution. These come from differences in the structure of the two languages. Sentences may be put together differently. Adjectives may follow instead of preceding the noun they modify. French nouns have masculine or feminine gender, and other words modifying or referring to a noun are found to have special endings to agree with the noun. Likewise, tenses do not have a one-to-one correspondence. The French, by using different tenses, make a distinction as to whether or not a past activity was completed. These and similar problems presented by the structure of French lie outside the scope of the dictionary. It is possible to know the exact meaning and even the precise translation of each word and still be unable to combine these elements in any way that will convey the sense of the original. In order to cope with this type of difficulty, one must master the basic structure of the language. That is what is presented here. This book provides students of science and engineering with the briefest explanation of the structural aspects of technical French that will permit them to translate papers of normal difficulty accurately and completely into English.

When the primary aim is reading, one is interested in understanding the forms that occur in a passage. But the traditional language textbook aims at telling how to reproduce these forms for use in speaking or writing. This book is written from the reader's point of view. It answers such questions as: "How do I know whether the form before me is subject or object of the verb?" instead of answering the grammarian's question: "How do I form the accusative from the nominative form I have already learned?" In short, the aim here is analytic, rather than synthetic.

A perennial difficulty in beginner's language texts is grammatical terminology. No discussion of the structure of a language is possible without it, yet the average person is rarely familiar with it. Hence all grammatical terms are explained when they are introduced, and the number is kept to a minimum.

It may not be obvious that reading in a foreign language is an acquired skill of the highest order. It takes extensive practice. This book and the dictionary are the tools for the job, but to acquire any facility you must read one hundred or two hundred pages of material on various aspects of your field written by different authors, and then go on reading year after year, using and improving your skill.

Thanks are hereby expressed to copyright owners for their kind permission to use the material in the Exercises.

Table 4 is reproduced from *French Word Book* by G. Vander Beke, Macmillan (1929), by permission of the copyright owners, the American Council on Education, and the Bureau of Educational Research, University of Wisconsin.

WILLIAM N. LOCKE

December, 1956

Contents

Lesson

1 Pronunciation, Nasal Vowels, General Hints on Pronunciation, Hints on Comprehension   **1**

2 Translation, Word Order, Elision; Commonest Words in French   **10**

3 Verbs—Principal Parts, Regular and Irregular Verbs; Common Verbs; Reflexive Verbs   **17**

4 Tenses of Verbs, Tense Endings of Regular Verbs, Meanings of Simple Tenses, Formation of Compound Tenses, Meanings of Compound Tenses   **25**

5 Questions, Inverted Word Order, Articles   **35**

6 Pronouns: (*A*) Used with Verb, (*B*) Emphatic, (*C*) Relative   **44**

7 Pronouns: (*D*) Demonstrative and Demonstrative Adjectives, (*E*) Possessive Adjectives and Pronouns   **53**

8 Comparisons, Negative Expressions   **62**

9 Interrogative Adjectives and Pronouns, (*F*) Indefinite
   Interrogative Pronouns; Numbers: Cardinal, Ordinal,
   Decimals, Fractions; *Devoir, Savoir* and *Pouvoir*　　**71**

10 Idiomatic Expressions, Use of *Faire, Convenir*　　**81**

11 Plurals of Nouns and Adjectives; Gender of Nouns, of
    Adjectives; Spelling of Verbs　　**88**

Appendix

1 The Subjunctive, Tenses of the Subjunctive　　**95**

2 Conjugation of *Avoir* and *Etre*　　**103**

3 Alphabetical List of Irregular Verb Forms　　**108**

Pronunciation

French is similar to English in large portions of its vocab-
ulary and in word order, but in pronunciation it is radically dif-

TABLE 1. LETTERS ALWAYS REPRESENTING SIMILAR SOUNDS
IN ENGLISH AND FRENCH

(Illustrated by Similar Sounding Words)

LETTER	ENGLISH	FRENCH	(MEANING OF FRENCH)
b	bell	bel	(fine, handsome)
d	deem	dîme	(tithe)
f	fool	foule	(crowd)
k	kangaroo	kangourou	(kangaroo)
l	lack	lac	(lake)
p	peak	pic	(peak, pick)
s ("s" sound)	see	si	(if, yes)
s ("z" sound)	rose	rose	(rose)
t	tell	telle	(such)
v	valor	valeur	(value)
x	ax	axe	(axis, axle)
z	zone	zône	(zone)

ferent. Because of this difference, French pronunciation needs special study to be understood or imitated. The ear has to be trained to catch French sounds, and English speaking habits have to be profoundly modified to produce them.

In the tables in this lesson the sounds represented by French letters are illustrated by the nearest American equivalent; this approximation often will not give a pronunciation understandable to a Frenchman, but may be sufficient for the communication of French words between Americans.*

TABLE 2. LETTERS SOMETIMES REPRESENTING SIMILAR SOUNDS
IN FRENCH AND ENGLISH

(See Other Uses of These Letters in Table 3)

LETTER	ENGLISH	FRENCH	(MEANING OF FRENCH)
a	ah	a	(has)
c (= k before a, o, or u)	cam	came	(cam)
c (= s before e, i, or y)	censure	censure	(censorship)
e	bell	bel	(fine, handsome)
g (= g before a, o, or u)	gum	gomme	(gum)
m	meal	mille	(thousand)
n	knee	ni	(neither, nor)
o	boss	bosse	(bump, knob, stud)
o	no	nos	(our)
qu (= k)	bouquet	bouquet	(bouquet)
y	Yugoslavia	Yougoslavie	(Yugoslavia)
ou	soup	soupe	(soup)

---

* For the sounds of French, listen to *Introduction to French Speech Habits,* three records by Pierre Delattre (Henry Holt and Co.). Continue with *Spoken French,* twelve records by Denoeu (Holt).

TABLE 3a. LETTERS REPRESENTING DIFFERENT SOUNDS
IN FRENCH AND ENGLISH

LETTER	ENGLISH	FRENCH	(MEANING OF FRENCH)
ch	*sh*ows	*ch*ose	(thing)
e (1)	The *e* part of *her*, without any *r* quality	le	(the, him, or it)
'e, ai (2)	Both alike; no English sound; somewhat similar to the *a* in *fate*	les; fait	(the, them; fact)
e, ai, ei (3)	All alike; similar to the *e* in *bell*	bref; faible; beige	(brief, short; weak, slight; beige
g (before *e, i*, or y)	Sound of *z* in *azure*	âge	(age)
gn	Sound of *ny* as in *canyon*	signe	(sign)
i	A much sharper, higher *ee* sound than in the English *feet*	ici	(here)
j	Same as *g*, above, like *z* in *azure*	je	(I)
r	A guttural sound not used in American English, similar to German *r* and Spanish *j*	Paris	(Paris)
u	A sound not known in America. Pronounced by holding tongue in position for *ee*, rounding and protruding lips	du	(some)
w	Usually *v* sound, rarely *w*	wagon	(railroad car)

[1] Other spellings of this sound are *-ez, -et, -er,* or *-e* followed by any unpronounced consonant at the end of a word.

TABLE 3a. (Continued)

LETTER	ENGLISH	FRENCH	(MEANING OF FRENCH)
au	Same as ô, but not lengthened, similar to the o part of *bowl*	au	(to the, at the, etc.)
eu	Similar to the e of *her*, without the r but with lips pursed	leur	(to them, their)
oi	oi has sound of *wah*	moi	(me, to me, rarely I)

TABLE 3b. FRENCH LETTERS NOT USED IN ENGLISH

LETTER	NEAREST ENGLISH EQUIVALENT	FRENCH WORD	(MEANING OF FRENCH)
à	ah	à	(to, at, in)
â	ah	âge	(age)
ç	*so*	leçon	(lesson)
[1]é	somewhat like *a* in *able*	état	(state)
[2]ê [2]è	similar to the e in *bell*	{ être près	(to be) (near)
î	used mostly in conjunction with a where aî represents the same sound as ê, above: *naître*—to be born. Also found in oî, pronounced like oi, and in uî, pronounced like u + i run together in a diphthong: *boîte*—box; *huître*—oyster.		
ô	similar to the o part of *bowl*	côte	(coast)
ù	used in the word où (where) to distinguish it from ou (or); same sound as u in Table 3a.		
û	same sound as u in Table 3a.		

The accent marks have two different uses in French; sometimes they simply distinguish one word from another, à (to) from a (has). They more frequently indicate different vowel sounds and are then best treated as separate letters.

The accent mark (ˆ) over the last vowel in a word means that the sound is lengthened, lasting roughly twice as long as most vowels.

---

[1] Same sound as e, ei, (2) in Table 3a.

[2] Same sound as e, ai, ei, (3) in Table 3a.

NASAL VOWELS

In French there are four vowel sounds which are pronounced in such a way that the sound comes out through the nose as well as the mouth. We also have such sounds. The *a* of *can* and the *a* of *cat* sound quite different, but in English they are not recognized as separate vowels. In French they are.

In English the *m* or *n* which causes the vowel to have a nasal sound is invariably pronounced. In French the *m* or *n* is written after the nasal vowels but never pronounced.

Four French vowels have a nasal sound when followed by *m* or *n*, before another consonant or at the end of a word. They are: (1) *e* as in *let*, (2) *a* as in *ah*, (3) *o* as in the *o* of *bowl*, and (4) *eu* as in *her*, without an *r* sound and with lips pursed. As seen in the tables above, there are many spellings for these four sounds. Each of their nasal counterparts also has numerous spellings:

VOWELS	NASAL COUNTERPARTS
1. e	ein, eim, ain, aim, in, im, yn, ym
2. a	an, am, en, em
3. o	on, om
4. eu	eun, un, um

As for the sound of these nasal vowels, no. 1 is similar to the nasal vowel in English *can* without the consonant *n*. The others have no resemblance to any English sound.

It is emphasized that a French vowel is nasal only if it is followed by *m* or *n* at the end of a word or if the *m* or *n* is followed by another consonant; the *m* or *n* is then silent. At the beginning of a word or between vowels, or when *mm* or *nn* is written, *m* or *n* is sounded as in English and the preceding vowel is not nasal.

GENERAL HINTS ON PRONUNCIATION

In English each main word has one or more accents. *Opportu-nity* has an accent on alternate syllables. In French there is no analogous use of accent or stress. The accent marks on vowels never indicate the presence of stress. A melodic variation, consisting of higher or lower tone, and a lengthening of the last vowel of a word or phrase take the place of accent as we know it in English. *Opportunité* has even stress throughout, but the *é* is pronounced on a different tone and lengthened.

Questions are asked with rising inflection and the voice is dropped at the end of a statement as in English.

Two or more adjacent vowels are pronounced in one utterance so that the speaker glides from one to the other without the slightest break.

When a French word ends in a consonant, the chances are that the consonant will not be pronounced. There is a rule, though it has exceptions, that *c, r, f,* and *l* are pronounced when they come at the end of one-syllable words.

The pronunciation of *e* presents special difficulties. Whenever it is followed by one or more pronounced consonants in the same syllable, it has the sound of *è*. Otherwise it is usually silent when it is in the middle or at the end of a polysyllabic word. In one-syllable words like *le,* it is often dropped in rapid speech.

h is never pronounced. Most words beginning with *h* are treated as though the *h* were not there. In a few, the memory of the *h* influences the pronunciation of the preceding word.

Double consonants sound like single consonants, except *s,* where one *s* between vowels is pronounced *z* and double *ss* indicates the *s* sound. Cf. *composé* (compound) vs. *possible* (possible).

Groups of words closely linked by meaning, such as modifiers with their noun or verb, or pronoun subject and verb, are pronounced like a single word. Hence, there occur some changes in pronunciation within such a group. This partially accounts for the difficulty of understanding spoken French even after one can read it.

HINTS ON COMPREHENSION

The American student of scientific French is particularly fortunate because he can readily recognize a large proportion of the words he will meet. The common Latin and Greek backgrounds of the two languages make it relatively easy to guess the correct meaning of thousands of words.

Many words not identical in spelling have several syllables which are alike; the root of the word, minus prefix and suffix, may be known. Then there are certain correspondences which are helpful for intelligent guessing. The prefix *dé-* often corresponds to "de-," "dis-," or "un-." The letter *é-* beginning a French word often stands for an "s" in English (*étoffe* = stuff, cloth). *o* and *ou* may change place in the two languages (*poche* = pouch, *couleur* = color).

Certain suffixes often correspond in the two languages:

SUFFIXES		EXAMPLES
FRENCH	ENGLISH	
-aire	-ary	*ordinaire*, ordinary
-eur	-or	*tenseur*, tensor
-euse	-er	*laveuse*, washer, washing machine
-eux	-ous	*ferreux*, ferrous
-ic	-ic	*arsenic*, arsenic
-ique	-ic	*borique*, boric
-ment	-ly	*rapidement*, rapidly
-oire	-ory	*accessoire*, accessory
-té	-ty	*cavité*, cavity
-ure	-ide	*chlorure*, chloride

It is suggested that you write out a translation into good technical English of each of the sample sentences and exercises in this book. Use your dictionary.* In the early lessons, not all the difficulties in the exercises will have been covered. This is inevitable since the exercises are unsimplified material, taken directly from the source indicated.

EXERCISE

Représentation Graphique. Un tableau numérique tel que celui que nous avons établi précédemment donne déjà nettement *l'allure d'une fonction,* c'est-à-dire la façon dont la fonction *varie avec la variable.*

Mais la représentation graphique est, à ce point de vue, bien meilleure, elle permet de juger *d'un coup d'oeil* l'allure de la fonction.

En général, on prend un système de deux axes de *coordonnées* rectangulaires.

Sur un axe, axe des *abscisses,* on porte des longueurs proportionnelles aux valeurs de la *variable.*

Sur l'autre axe, axe des *ordonnées,* on porte des longeurs proportionnelles aux valeurs de la *fonction.*

Si, par exemple, nous devons représenter graphiquement le tableau précédent, nous portons, sur l'axe des abscisses, des longueurs proportionnelles aux valeurs des températures et, sur l'axe des ordonnées, des longueurs proportionnelles aux valeurs des volumes. Autrement dit, de façon plus concise, nous portons les températures sur l'axe des abscisses et les volumes sur l'axe des ordonnées.

Il n'est pas nécessaire que le coefficient de proportionnalité entre ces longueurs et ces valeurs soit le même pour les deux axes, autrement dit que les deux *échelles* adoptées pour les deux axes soient les mêmes.

---

* For scientists, Patterson: *French-English Dictionary for Chemists* (Wiley), 2nd edition, 1954, is suggested. For engineers, DeVries: *French-English Science Dictionary* (McGraw-Hill). Specialized bilingual dictionaries exist for numerous fields. Some are excellent, others are very poor.

Si nous nous servons d'un papier *millimétré*, nous admettons, par exemple, qu'un centimètre sur l'axe des abscisses correspond à un écart de température de 5° (échelle 2 millimètres par degré) et qu'un centimètre sur l'axe des ordonnées correspond à un écart de volume de $0^l, 10$ (échelle 10 centimètres par litre).

Si nous nous servons d'un simple papier quadrillé, nous admettons qu'une division sur l'axe des abscisses correspond à un écart de température de 5° et qu'une division sur l'axe des ordonnées correspond à un écart de volume de $0^l, 10$.

Il n'est pas nécessaire d'ailleurs que l'origine des coordonnées corresponde à des valeurs nulles de la variable et de la fonction.

Alors, on porte, sur les axes des coordonnées, des longueurs non plus proportionnelles aux valeurs de la variable et de la fonction, mais proportionnelles aux variations de ces deux grandeurs, à partir de valeurs arbitrairement choisies pour chacune d'elles.—L. Gay, *Mathématiques du Chimiste,* Paris, Hermann, 1926, pp. 35–37.

Translation

Scientific French is much like scientific English; so it is far easier to read than literary French. In general, one sentence in the French corresponds to one sentence in English; a clause to a clause, a phrase to a phrase; and in the great majority of cases, an English word can be found to express each French word. Perhaps this situation seems so natural that it should be taken for granted. Yet in Russian where there are no articles and few prepositions, or in the Far Eastern languages where modes of expression are still more different from ours, it would be impossible to proceed on this assumption.

For any language it is impossible to rely on word-for-word correspondence for translation. Such a translation will usually be sufficient to give a crude idea of the intent of the original author. It will not be English. It is a first step. The second and essential step involves turning the rough approximation into good English with the same meaning as the original. In short, you cannot translate words. Translation means restating ideas in another language.

Fortunately, as a result of our common intellectual background, our ways of expressing ideas are very similar to French ways.

That is why French, especially technical French, is easy for Americans to learn.

WORD ORDER

The order of words in French statements is much like that of English: subject + verb + objects, with the direct object before the indirect object. This is true of most statements where the objects are both nouns. For example: *Elle peut . . . donner lieu à un équilibre* = It may . . . give rise to an equilibrium.

In French where the objects are pronouns they come between the subject and verb. There is no word for *to*, as there usually is with the English indirect object (to him, to her) to guide one in knowing which object is the one to which one gives the thing, for example, but many of the pronoun objects have different forms for the direct and indirect object uses (*le* = him; *lui* = to him). In a statement with pronoun objects, the French order is subject + object + verb: *Il les prend* = He takes them.

For questions in both languages, the subject may follow the verb. Examples will be given later. Also in commands, our usage is like the French: *brisez en morceaux* = break into pieces; *prenez un cas type* = take a typical case; *qu'il parte* = let it start (leave).

Perhaps the most striking divergence in word order occurs in the position of adjectives. In English the adjective usually precedes the noun it modifies. In French the adjective usually follows its noun: *éléments chimiques, conditions physiques, d'une manière continue*. But the Exercise at the end of this lesson, from which these examples are taken, shows that there are many cases where adjectives precede nouns: *une même substance, mêmes éléments, diverses formes*. The short, common adjectives often precede; long adjectives almost invariably follow their noun. Articles like *un* (= a) and *le* (= the) always precede. Technical adjectives follow, for instance: *acide chlorhydrique* = hydrochloric acid; *la classification périodique* = the periodic table.

In English most nouns may be used as adjectives, greatly simplifying terminology. The French often have to use the noun with *de* (of) as in the following:

ENGLISH		FRENCH	
K_2CO_3	potassium carbonate	carbonate de potassium	CO_3K_2
$Na_2S_2O_3 \cdot 5H_2O$	sodium hyposulphite	hyposulphite de sodium	$S_2O_3Na_25H_2O$
$Al(C_6H_5CO_2)_3$	aluminum benzoate	benzoate d'aluminium	$(C_6H_5CO_2)_3Al$

Note how the French often carry over the word order into the terms of the formula. In recent years they tend to conform to international standards so that, more and more, the order of terms is becoming the same as ours. It should be mentioned also that the French formerly used superscripts where we use subscripts. Here, too, they are gradually adopting the more general usage.

ELISION

In *benzoate d'aluminium,* above, the *-e* of *de* has disappeared before a vowel at the beginning of a following word. In the Exercise examples of *l'* and *c'* show the same phenomenon. French monosyllables ending in *-e*, (*ce, de, je, le, me, ne, que, se, te*), drop the *-e* and replace it with an apostrophe before a vowel at the beginning of a following word. The two words are then pronounced as one. The only exceptions to this rule are the infrequent cases where *ce, je,* or *le* follow a verb, being its subject or object: *est-ce un principe?* (is it a principle?); *divisez-le* (divide it). No trouble should be caused to the translator by the elisions. The meaning remains clear.

Two other cases of elision should be mentioned. The article and pronoun *la* (= the, it, her) loses its *-a*, just as the words above lose *-e*. *La* is the only word in which *-a* may be elided. As a result, *l'état* could stand either for *la* or *le* + *état* (actually it is the latter, since *état* is masculine). The vowel *i* is apparently elided in *s'il*, but this really comes from *se* + *il* at an earlier period when *se* was used for "if." Today "if" is *si*, but with *il* the old elision still subsists: *s'il* (if it, if he).

Table 4. The Commonest Words in French

Listed below are the words occurring most frequently in ordinary French, as determined by a word count of 400,000 running words of French prose. The figures after each word indicate its average number of occurrences per 1,000 words. It will be seen that the total is 446.1. In other words, learn these and you know 44.6% of the words of French. Learn them now.

The meanings given are the commonest English translations. Others are possible.

à, au, aux, à l' = to, at, in, to the, at the, in the	21.4
aller = to go	2.1
autre = other	1.7
avec = with	3.4
[1]avoir = to have	13.7
bien (adv.) = well, very	2.8
bon = good	1.2
ce, cet, cette = this, that ces = these, those	12.0
comme = as, like	2.5
dans = in, within	6.7
de, du, de l', de la, des = of, from, of the, from the	54.9
deux = two	1.8
dire = to say, tell	4.2
[1]donner = to give	1.4
elle; elles = she, it, her; they, them	8.0
en (prep.) = in, while	6.3
en (pron.) = of it, of them, some, in the matter	2.6
enfant = child	1.1
et = and	19.1
[1]être (v.) = to be	20.6
	187.5

[1]faire = to make, do, have (something done)	4.5
femme = woman, wife	1.2
grand = tall, big	2.0
homme = man, husband	2.4
il; ils = he, it, him; they, them	13.7
[2]je = I	
jour = day	1.2
le, la, l', les (art.) = the le, la, l', les (pron.) = him, her, it, them	69.4
leur (pron.) = to them, them leur, -s (adj.) = their	2.6
lui (pron.) = (to) him, her, it	3.8
mais = but	3.7
[2]me = me, to me	
[2]moi = me, I	15.0
mon, ma, mes (adj.) = my	4.5
ne . . . pas = not	10.5
notre, nos = our	1.2
nous = we, us, to us	4.1
on = one, they, we	3.9
	143.7

TABLE 4. (Continued)

ou = or		se = himself, herself, itself,	
ou . . . ou = either }	1.9	oneself, themselves, each	
. . . or		other	8.7
où = where	1.1	si = if, even if }	2.5
par = by	3.7	si = so	
pas (neg. adv.) = not, no	5.6	son, sa, ses = his, her, its	8.9
petit = little, small	1.7	sur (prep.) = on	3.4
plus (adv.) = more	4.3	tout = all, every	6.1
pour = for, in order to	3.2	tu, te, toi = you	1.8
[1]pouvoir (v.) = to be able, can	1.9	un, une (art.) = a, an } un (num.) = one	18.5
[2]prendre = to take	1.2	[1]venir = to come	1.3
que (conj.) = as, than	12.8	[1]voir = to see	2.1
que? (interr.) = what } que (rel. pron.) = who, whom, which, that	3.0	votre, vos = your	1.3
qui? (interr.) = who? } qui (rel. pron.) = who, whom, which, that	7.6	[1]vouloir (v.) = to want, wish	1.5
		vous = you, to you	5.2
sans = without	1.8	y = to it, to them, in it, in them, there	2.4
[1]savoir (v.) = to know	1.4		63.7
	51.2		187.5
			143.7
			51.2
		Total—446.1	

---

[1] The various forms of the verb were combined in the count.

[2] These words were combined in the count, giving 15.0, listed after *moi*.

SAMPLE SENTENCES

Note. Always read each sentence through, using your knowledge of English and of the general context to get a feel for the whole before starting to assign meanings to individual words.

1. Il est admis tacitement que les particules nous arrivent individuellement.

2. Le fait intéressant à retenir est le suivant.

3. Ces expériences nous apportent des éléments intéressants relatifs à la détermination du type réel de structure cristalline de MnO_2.

4. Le centre de gravité d'un corps est le point où se trouve appliquée la résultante de toutes les forces p, p', p'' . . . exercées par la pesanteur sur les divers fragments constitutifs du corps.

5. Des expériences précédentes ont conduit à formuler une hypothèse sur l'existence des couches pelliculaires électro-aériennes constituées à l'image des condensateurs électriques.

6. Les explosions nucléaires observées dans les émulsions photographiques laissent désormais présumer qu'une fraction du rayonnement cosmique primaire consiste en particules multiples.

7. Il est à remarquer qu'un maximum du liquidus indique un produit qui fond à température constante.

8. L'identification des isotopes est difficile, ce qui entraîne une incertitude sur A.

9. Il est vrai que dans ce cas, il admet l'intervention puissante de nombreux autres facteurs interférents, en particulier la mémoire des images, la sensibilisation par les hormones, les phénomènes d'inhibition.

10. Considérons un cadre circulaire, mobile autour d'un axe vertical.

EXERCISE

Une même substance, composée des mêmes éléments chimiques, peut se présenter sous diverses formes. Lorsque les conditions physiques, et notamment la température et la ¯pression, varient d'une manière continue, les propriétés de la substance, en général, varient aussi d'une manière continue. On convient de dire alors que la *forme* ou *l'état* de la substance restent les mêmes. Mais il peut arriver que, pour une certaine température et une certaine pression, toutes les propriétés de la substance

changent brusquement, par une transformation discontinue.
Durant la transformation, il y a une limite nette, strictement
définie, entre la partie transformée et celle qui ne l'est pas encore.
Ces deux portions de la substance se comportent comme deux
phases distinctes, et peuvent être physiquement aussi différentes
entre elles que deux substances chimiquement différentes. La
transformation peut se faire hors d'équilibre. Elle peut aussi, et
c'est le cas ordinaire, donner lieu à un équilibre. Elle est alors
réversible, et se produit à une température qui est fonction de la
pression, suivant les lois thermodynamiques connues. Le type
classique de ces transformations discontinues, c'est celle qui se
produit au *point de fusion*.—GEORGES FRIEDEL, *Leçons de cristallographie*, Paris, Berger-Levrault, 1926, p. XVI.

Verbs—Principal Parts

The principal parts of a verb are so chosen as to show all the peculiarities of the stem of the verb as it is used to form various tenses. If the principal parts are known, it is possible to recognize the infinitive to which any form belongs; then the meaning can be looked up in the dictionary. But if one does not know the principal parts of a verb, it may be impossible, even with a good dictionary, to know what a particular verb form means. Verbs like *saura, faille, ira* are not found in their alphabetical place in a dictionary; they are grouped under their infinitives: *savoir, falloir, aller.*

We shall use seven principal parts, as follows: infinitive, present participle, past participle, present indicative, present subjunctive, past definite, and future. They are illustrated with forms of *aller* = "to go."

1. *Infinitive* (*aller*)—The infinitive is the part of a verb most often used as a noun, also the part listed in dictionaries. In English the infinitive is usually given in the form accompanied by the preposition "to," as "to go." In French various prepositions may precede the infinitive, the commonest being *à* or *de* but there may be none. The question of whether a preposition is used be-

fore an infinitive, or which preposition, is a matter of the preceding word or words, those on which the infinitive depends; for instance, *il a à aller* = he has to go; *il veut aller* = he wants to go; *il refuse d'aller* = he refuses to go. The use or omission of "to" in English before an infinitive also depends on the preceding or governing words.

The infinitive is often used as an imperative: *Ne pas laisser tomber* = Do not drop.

2. *Present Participle (allant)*—This is the "-ing" form of the verb, used mainly after the preposition *en* in such expressions as *en allant* = while going, on going, or, going. The English use of the present participle is far more extensive than the French use: Seeing is believing = *Voir c'est croire*. In French we find the infinitive after other verbs, where we may use a participle: *il commence à bouillir* = it begins boiling (or "to boil"); *il voit partir le train* = he sees the train leaving (or "leave").

3. *Past Participle (allé)*—This is the "-ed" form of the verb, or the form used to make compound tenses: had cooled (*avait refroidi*), has opened (*a ouvert*), etc. The French past participle is also widely used as an adjective: *la somme due* = the sum due; *la décision une fois prise . . .* = once the decision has (or had) been made. . . .

4. *Present Indicative (va)*—This is the present tense which shows action now or action considered as independent of time: *deux fois deux font quatre* = two times two makes four; *il est* = it is.

5. *Present Subjunctive (aille)*—The present subjunctive is a tense which is quite limited in its uses. In the third person singular (*Soit x = 3*—Let *x* = 3, or, *Qu'il aille!*—Let him go!) it constitutes an imperative. For the rest, it is used in subordinate clauses after "which" and "that." The great majority of these cases express no idea which could not equally well be expressed by the indicative tenses. Certain verbs and conjunctions traditionally require the subjunctive in a following subordinate clause. In

translation the subjunctive form may be treated like an indicative of the same tense.

6. *Past Definite* (*alla*)—This is a tense which is gradually disappearing from use. It is no longer used in conversation and informal writing; even in formal writing it is beginning to be replaced by the compound past (*il est allé* = he went). However, the past definite tense is the traditional tense for stating events which took place in the past. It will be found in formal reports, books, and even newspapers.

7. *Future* (*ira*)—In English there is no future form. We express the future by joining the present tense of the auxiliary verbs "shall" or "will" with the infinitive of the verb. We say: "I will (or shall) go." The French form the future of regular verbs by taking the infinitive and adding to it a set of endings identical to the present tense of *avoir* except that the *av-* of *avons* and *avez* is dropped as is the *-e* of infinitives ending in *-re* (*vendre* gives *vendrai*, *vendra*, etc., in the future). What the Frenchman says is: *je donnerai* = I shall give (*je donner+ai*, literally, "I to give have").

In *ira* we see one of relatively few irregular futures. Instead of adding the future endings to *aller*, the infinitive, the French use an older alternate infinitive, *ir*, as the stem.

Note that principal parts 4–7 are actually representative forms of tenses. These are the tenses where irregularities of stem most often occur. The form used with *il* or *elle* is the one given.

REGULAR AND IRREGULAR VERBS

Ninety percent of French verbs are regular. That is, the body of the word remains the same while endings are changed to indicate different tenses. Table 5 on the following pages gives the principal parts of three regular verbs and of thirty irregular verbs. The three regular verbs represent the majority of French verbs, which are of three types, as described in the following lesson.

TABLE 5. COMMON

INFINITIVE	PRESENT PARTICIPLE	PAST PARTICIPLE
		Regular
donner (to give)	donnant (giving)	donné (given)
finir (to finish)	finissant	fini
vendre (to sell)	vendant	vendu
		Irregular
aller (to go)	allant	allé
[3]avoir (to have)	ayant	eu
boire (to drink)	buvant	bu
connaître (to know)	connaissant	connu
croire (to believe)	croyant	cru
devoir (to have to[2])	devant	dû
dire (to say)	disant	dit
écrire (to write)	écrivant	écrit
envoyer (to send)	envoyant	envoyé
[3]être (to be)	étant	été
faire (to make)	faisant	fait
falloir (to be necessary)	(no pres. part.)	fallu
lire (to read)	lisant	lu
mettre (to put)	mettant	mis
mourir (to die)	mourant	mort
naître (to be born)	naissant	né
ouvrir (to open)	ouvrant	ouvert
partir (to leave)	partant	parti
pleuvoir (to rain)	pleuvant	plu
pouvoir (to be able)	pouvant	pu
prendre (to take)	prenant	pris
recevoir (to receive)	recevant	reçu
rire (to laugh)	riant	ri
savoir (to know)	sachant	su
venir (to come)	venant	venu
voir (to see)	voyant	vu
vouloir (to wish)	voulant	voulu

PRESENT INDICATIVE	PRESENT SUBJUNCTIVE	PAST DEFINITE	FUTURE
Verbs			
donne (gives)	donne (give)	donna (gave)	donnera (will give)
finit	finisse	finit	finira
vend	vende	vendit	vendra
Verbs			
va	aille	alla	ira
a	ait	eut	aura
boit	boive	but	[1]
connaît	connaisse	connut	[1]
croit	croie	crut	[1]
doit	doive	dut	devra
dit	dise	dit	[1]
écrit	écrive	écrivit	[1]
envoie	envoie	envoya	enverra
est	soit	fut	sera
fait	fasse	fit	fera
faut	faille	fallut	faudra
lit	lise	lut	[1]
met	mette	mit	[1]
meurt	meure	mourut	mourra
naît	naisse	naquit	[1]
ouvre	ouvre	ouvrit	[1]
part	parte	partit	[1]
pleut	pleuve	plut	pleuvra
peut	puisse	put	pourra
prend	prenne	prit	[1]
reçoit	reçoive	reçut	recevra
rit	rie	rit	[1]
sait	sache	sut	saura
vient	vienne	vint	viendra
voit	voie	vit	verra
veut	veuille	voulut	voudra

[1] Formed regularly, infinitive plus future endings.

[2] Additional meanings of various tenses: must, ought to, should, to be to, to owe.

[3] For complete list of the forms of *avoir* and *être,* see Appendix II.

The three regular verbs given in the above table are representative of all the regular verbs. Unfortunately for the learner, the irregular verbs are among the most commonly used. Several of the latter figure in the Table of Commonest Words in French, Table 4. It will be essential for you to know every one of the forms in Table 5. Without them, you can never have any facility in translating French.

REFLEXIVE VERBS

Most reflexive verbs, i.e., verbs whose subject and object refer to the same person or thing (he hurts himself—*il se blesse*), will be identified readily by the presence of the object pronoun *se* (*s'* before a vowel). The use of reflexives is far more common in French than in English and it is frequently necessary to translate it by a non-reflexive, for example *il se met en mouvement*—it starts to move (literally, it puts itself in motion). For more details and other reflexive constructions, see pp. 32 and 44-46.

SAMPLE SENTENCES

Pay special attention to the verbs which are in italics.

1. Naturellement, ces trois axes *sont tracés* non plus sur un plan, mais dans l'espace.

2. Pour *étudier* les courants de convection dans une nappe liquide, j'ai *choisi* la même uniformité de conditions dans le plan horizontal.

3. J'*ai cherché* à réaliser un tel dispositif en *éliminant* toute influence de paroi latérale.

4. Le ciel supérieur et moyen est *déterminé* par les processus thermodynamiques *liés* aux grandes perturbations atmosphériques.

5. La question ainsi *posée*, détails *mis* à part, *appartient* au problème général des ondes de canaux.

6. Il *faut retirer* la nourriture au bout de quelques heures pour *éviter* une altération de l'eau.

7. L'observateur *devra* donc *s'efforcer* de porter sur le ciel *observé* un jugement synthétique.

8. On aura pour tout point de cette région l'égalité, *P étant* un contour *fermé* simple *enveloppant* le cercle *c*.

EXERCISE

Write out a translation into good technical English. If the job is well done, no one should be able to tell from your English that it is a translation.

Il n'est guère de mots qui semblent correspondre à une notion plus claire et plus simple que l'expression *point de fusion*. Et cependant, si l'on y regarde de plus près, il en est peu qui soient plus mal choisis et de nature à créer ou perpétuer plus d'idées fausses.

Le mot *fusion* implique qu'il s'agit du passage d'un état solide à un état liquide. Prenons un corps cristallisé franchement solide, le sel gemme à la température ordinaire, par exemple. Élevons la température. A 776°, sous la pression atmosphérique, nous verrons se produire la transformation discontinue, réversible, qui constitue la fusion. Mais dans cette transformation il se produit en réalité deux choses: d'une part, la matière passe d'un état nettement solide à un état nettement liquide; d'autre part, elle passe de l'état cristallisé à l'état amorphe. Ces deux caractères du *point de fusion* sont-ils toujours simultanés, et si non, auquel correspond la discontinuité?

Pour répondre à ces questions, choisissons d'autres exemples. Le verre à vitres ordinaire est, à la température habituelle, amorphe et solide. Élevons la température. Nous verrons, sans aucune discontinuité, sans qu'on puisse observer à aucune température une limite naturelle qui s'impose, le corps devenir graduellement plus pâteux, puis arriver à un état franchement liquide. La physique peut bien définir convenablement l'état solide et l'état liquide lorsqu'ils sont très caractérisés, mais elle reste impuissante à fixer entre ces deux états une limite qui ne soit pas arbitraire.—GEORGES FRIEDEL, *Leçons de cristallographie,* Paris, Berger-Levrault, 1926, pp. xvi–xvii.

Tenses of Verbs

The various tenses show the different times when the action of the verb happens, happened, or will happen, for example. In English we use endings added to the stem of the verb, as the "-s" for present happenings and "-ed" for past, but we use relatively few tenses formed this way. For the future we put the infinitive after "will." For the conditional "would" and "should" are used as auxiliary verbs with the infinitive: "would happen." Then there are the so-called compound tenses: "it has happened, had happened, might have happened," etc.

In French there are many more tenses formed by adding endings, generally a different set of endings for each tense. The endings in each set change also according to whether the subject is singular or plural and whether it is in the first person (I, we), second person (you), or third person (he, they). As if these two variables were not enough, there is a third: different sets of endings are used with various types of verbs in a few tenses (present indicative, present subjunctive, past definite, imperfect subjunctive). And a fourth: the stem or part of the verb to which the endings are added varies from tense to tense. Some tenses are formed from one principal part, some from another. Fortunately in regular verbs, which are by far the most numerous, the stem remains the same or almost the same in all the tenses (hence in all the principal parts) and complications are very much reduced.

The types of verbs mentioned above as requiring different sets of endings in a few tenses are identified by the ending of the infinitive. Most infinitives end in *-er*, some in *-ir*, and a few in *-re*. In Table 6 examples are given of the endings used for each of these three types of infinitives.

If you were planning to speak or write French, you would have to be able to form the various tenses for any verb you wished to use. If you plan only to read and translate, you have to recognize *which* tense of *what* verb you have before you. You identify the tense from the ending and the verb from the stem.

TABLE 6. TENSE ENDINGS OF REGULAR VERBS

1. TENSES IN WHICH ENDINGS VARY WITH TYPE OF INFINITIVE

(*a*) Present

Infinitive ending in:

-er	-ir	-re
Example:		
donner	*finir*	*vendre*
je donn*e* (I give)	je fin*is* (I finish)	je vend*s* (I sell)
il donn*e* (he gives)	il fin*it* (he finishes)	il vend (he sells)
nous donn*ons* (we give)	nous finiss*ons* (we finish)	nous vend*ons* (we sell)
vous donn*ez* (you give)	vous finiss*ez* (they finish)	vous vend*ez* (you sell)
ils donn*ent* (they give)	ils finiss*ent* (they finish)	ils vend*ent* (they sell)

Note a: The present may be said to be based on two principal parts: the *je* and *il* forms on part no. 4, present indicative; the *nous* and *vous* forms on the present participle, part no. 2 (the *-ant* of the participle being dropped off); and the *ils* form usually on the present indicative, sometimes on the present participle. It is only in irregular verbs that this matters.

Note b: The pronoun subjects represent the whole class of subjects of the same person and number which may be used with the form indicated.

(*b*) Imperative

Infinitive ending in:

-er	-ir	-re
Donn*ons* (Let's give)	Finiss*ons* (Let's finish)	Vend*ons* (Let's sell)
Donn*ez* (Give)	Finiss*ez* (Finish)	Vend*ez* (Sell)

Note: The imperative is based on the present participle, dropping the *-ant*. It is usually identical with the present tense. The imperative stems and endings are usually the same as the present tense. The difference between the two is seen by the absence or presence of a subject.

(*c*) Past Definite

Infinitive ending in:

	-er		-ir		-re
je	donn*ai* (I gave)	je	fin*is* (I finished)	je	vend*is* (I sold)
il	donn*a* (he gave)	il	fin*it* (he finished)	il	vend*it* (he sold)
nous	donn*âmes* (we gave)	nous	fin*îmes* (we finished)	nous	vend*îmes* (we sold)
vous	donn*âtes* (you gave)	vous	fin*îtes* (you finished)	vous	vend*îtes* (you sold)
ils	donn*èrent* (they gave)	ils	fin*irent* (they finished)	ils	vend*irent* (they sold)

Note: The *il* form of the past definite is principal part no. 6. The past definite is never used in conversation, but is found in formal writing.

It is gradually disappearing from use, as is the imperfect subjunctive.

(*d*) Imperfect Subjunctive

Infinitive ending in:

	-er		*-ir*		*-re*
je	donn*asse* (I might give)	je	fin*isse* (I might finish)	je	vend*isse* (I might sell)
il	donn*ât* (he might give)	il	fin*ît* (he might finish)	il	vend*ît* (he might sell)
nous	donn*assions* (we might give)	nous	fin*issions* (we might finish)	nous	vend*issions* (we might sell)
vous	donn*assiez* (you must give)	vous	fin*issiez* (you might finish)	vous	vend*issiez* (you might sell)
ils	donn*assent* (they might give	ils	fin*issent* (they might finish)	ils	vend*issent* (they might sell)

Note: The imperfect subjunctive is based on principal part no. **6** with different endings.

2. TENSES WITH ONLY ONE SET OF ENDINGS FOR ALL VERBS

(*a*) Imperfect

je donn*ais* (I gave)
il   donn*ait* (he gave)
nous donn*ions* (we gave)
vous donn*iez* (you gave)
ils donn*aient* (they gave)

(*b*) Present Subjunctive

je donn*e* (I may give)
il   donn*e* (he may give)
nous donn*ions* (we may give)
vous donn*iez* (you may give)
ils donn*ent* (they may give)

Note: The imperfect and present subjunctive are formed from the present participle; the *-ant* is dropped and the endings are added. The endings of the imperfect and present subjunctive never change, either in irregular or in regular verbs. The stems of irregular verbs rarely show changes in the imperfect, often in the present subjunctive.

(c) Future

je donner*ai* (I will, shall give)

il donner*a* (he will, shall give)

nous donner*ons* (we will, shall give)

vous donner*ez* (you will, shall give)

ils donner*ont* (they will, shall give)

(d) Conditional

je donner*ais* (I would, should give)

il donner*ait* (he would, should give)

nous donner*ions* (we would, should give)

vous donner*iez* (you would, should give)

ils donner*aient* (they would, should give)

Note: The future and conditional are formed on the infinitive as a stem, except that the -*e* of the -*re* infinitives is dropped off before the endings are added. (Example from *vendre: je vendrai* = I will sell; *je vendrais* = I should, would sell.)

The endings in Table 6 are those which are used with all the verbs in the French language except a dozen or so of the commonest irregular verbs and, even there, the deviations are minor.

Though it seems unlikely that the translator of technical material will ever see the forms of the second person singular pronoun *tu,* or the corresponding verbs, it may be mentioned in passing that the *tu* form is identical with the *je* form if the latter ends in -*s;* otherwise an -*s* is added to it. The only exception is the singular imperative where the typical -*s* is dropped in certain cases.

MEANINGS OF SIMPLE TENSES

Table 7 summarizes the names and meanings of the French tenses. Perhaps it may be worthwhile to point out that the word "tense" comes from the Latin for time: "tempus." Tenses are sometimes thought of as designating different times but they have added many other functions. Conventional patterns of structure nowadays often impose one or another tense regardless

TABLE 7. MEANINGS OF SIMPLE TENSES

TENSE	TIME INDICATED	EXAMPLE	TRANSLATION
'Present	present or general	il donne	it gives, does give, is giving
Present Subjunctive	present or general	il donne	it give, gives, may give, used to give, would give
Imperative	present or general	donnez	give
'Imperfect Indicative	past	il donnait	it gave, did give, etc.
Imperfect Subjunctive	past	il donnât	it might give, gave, etc.
Past Definite	past	il donna	it gave
'Future	future	il donnera	it will, shall give
Conditional	future with respect to past	il donnerait	it would, should give

of the temporal significance. For instance, when the subjunctive is used, it will be the present subjunctive if it accompanies a present or future tense in the main clause of the sentence and the imperfect subjunctive if it follows a past tense. (*il faut qu'on commence* . . . = we must begin . . . ; *il fallut qu'on commençât* . . . = we had to begin . . .). It takes some experience with these patterns to know which have significance for the translator. Most subjunctives are best treated as though they were the corresponding indicative tense.

FORMATION OF COMPOUND TENSES

Each of the simple tenses except the imperative has a corresponding compound tense. That is, the auxiliary is in the simple

MEANINGS OF COMPOUND TENSES

TENSE	TIME INDICATED	EXAMPLE	TRANSLATION
[1]Compound Past	previous to present	il a donné	it gave, has given
Perfect Subjunctive		il ait donné	it (may) have given
Pluperfect	previous to some other time in past	il avait donné	it had given
Pluperfect Subjunctive		il eût donné	it had given
Past Anterior		il eut donné	it had given
Future Perfect	previous to another future	il aura donné	it will, shall have given
Conditional Perfect	previous to a past time	il aurait donné	it would, should have given

---

[1] These are the tenses most frequently encountered in technical writing.

tense; a past participle is added; and that gives a compound tense showing time before that expressed by the simple tense. It is easier than it sounds and just like English. Take the past tense "has"; the corresponding compound tense is "has had." If you form the future of the auxiliary, i.e., "will have" and add the past participle "had" then you have the compound future "will have had." In French it works the same way: *il a*—it has; *il a eu* = it has had; *il avait* = it had; *il avait eu* = it had had; *il aura eu* = it will have had. *Il* may mean "he" or "it," a fact to be kept in mind in reading the table.

The above examples of compound tenses show how simple tenses of *avoir* are used to form the compound tenses of *donner*. This corresponds to the English use of forms of "have" to form the compound tenses. In French a few verbs are *être* instead. These verbs are of two types, first a group of a dozen or more intransitive verbs which show motion or a change of state (*aller, monter, venir,* etc.) and, in addition, all the verbs which happen to have a reflexive object, i.e., there is a pronoun object of the verb which refers to the same person or thing as the subject of that verb: I hit myself—*je me suis frappé;* the two gases mixed—*les deux gaz se sont mélangés.* Table 8 shows examples of compound tenses formed with *être.* Note particularly the translations and compare with the passive: *il est mélangé*—it is mixed, etc.

TABLE 8. COMPOUND TENSES FORMED WITH ETRE

INTRANSITIVE VERB		VERB WITH REFLEXIVE OBJECT	
[1] il est venu	it came, has come	[1] il s'est mélangé	it mixed
il soit venu	it may have come	il se soit mélangé	it may have mixed
il était venu	it had come	il s'était mélangé	it had mixed
il fût venu	it might have come	il se fût mélangé	it might have mixed
il fut venu	it had come	il se fut mélangé	it had mixed
il sera venu	it will have come	il se sera mélangé	it will have mixed
il serait venu	it would have come	il se serait mélangé	it would have mixed

[1] These are the tenses most frequently encountered in technical writing.

SAMPLE SENTENCES

1. On *verra* plus loin que toutes les poussières denses incorporées *finissent* par se déposer en petits tas ronds.

2. L'étude du mécanisme de libération de la protéinase à l'extérieur des cellules nous *a conduits* tout d'abord à *examiner* le comportement de cultures *faites* dans des milieux de composition différente.

3. Ainsi, par exemple, les larves Cypris de la Sacculine ne *peuvent* pas *se fixer* sur les poils du crabe qu'elles *vont infester*.

4. Les essais *furent pratiqués* sur trois moteurs à explosion à quatre cylindres.

5. Dans un tel champ, la métrique de l'espace ne *saurait être* euclidienne puisque la gravitation *dépend* des variations de la courbure de l'espace.

6. On *voit* d'abord que, s'il *existe* deux fonctions intégrales *jouissant* des propriétés *indiquées,* leur différence *se réduira* nécessairement à une constante.

7. Les considérations précédentes nous *amènent* à *conclure* que pour que l'équation (1) *définisse* une propagation d'onde, il *faut admettre* que deux solutions, *supposées* existantes et *caractérisant* le phénomène, *se raccordent.*

8. Le disparition du peracide à laquelle on *devait s'attendre,* puisque le système *contient* un excès d'aldéhyde qui *réagit* avec le peracide, est *survenue* beaucoup plus tard.

9. Au cours de ces recherches, nous *nous sommes heurtés* à de nombreuses difficultés, dont voici les principales.

10. M. H. Webster *s'est trompé* sur le sens même de la circulation des filets liquides.

EXERCISE

Dans l'évolution rapide qui nous a valu depuis soixante ans l'aviation et la T.S.F., le phonographe et le cinématographe, le four électrique et l'air liquide, le transport de la force à distance et les multiples applications de l'électricité, pour ne mentionner que les conquêtes les plus extraordinaires, quelle a été la part de la France? Quelles sont les inventions françaises qui ont vu le jour depuis l'avènement de la troisième République?

A une question posée sous une forme aussi étroite, il serait impossible de répondre. Pas plus en ce qui concerne les inventions qu'en ce qui touche les arts ou la science pure, un pays ne saurait s'isoler du reste du monde. Il y a eu des inventeurs français, et beaucoup, et des plus grands, mais il n'y a pas, ou presque pas, d'inventions purement françaises. Tous les peuples collaborent suivant leur génie propre à cette grande tâche qui vise l'accroissement du bien-être de l'humanité.

Souvent la même idée se présente presque simultanément à un grand nombre d'esprits dans les pays les plus divers. Elle est d'abord vague et imprécise, et les essais de réalisation échouent. Un temps s'écoule. Des progrès s'étant fait jour dans un domaine voisin, l'idée est reprise, souvent fort loin des lieux où elle était née. De nouvelles tentatives donnent quelques résultats encourageants, mais très imparfaits et sans valeur pratique. Alors de tous les pays surgissent des techniciens qui reprennent les expériences, modifient les appareils, jusqu'au jour où, grâce à un perfectionnement parfois insignifiant, l'invention apparaît comme utilisable. Sans doute évoluera-t-elle encore sans jamais atteindre un stade véritablement définitif, mais elle est enfin acquise à l'humanité. Une fois de plus l'esprit peut se prévaloir d'une conquête nouvelle sur les choses.

Mais à qui revient la gloire de l'invention? Est-ce à celui qui a eu la première idée ou tout au moins qui l'a fait connaître le premier? Est-ce à celui qui a tenté le premier de la réaliser ou encore à celui dont les essais ont semblé, pour la première fois, donner quelques résultats? Au contraire, doit-on rapporter tout le mérite à celui qui a su apporter à l'invention le perfectionnement qui devait la rendre viable?—A. Boutaric, *Les Grandes Inventions Françaises*, Paris, Editions de France, 1932, pp. 3–5.

Questions

Most questions in French are expressed the way they would be in English; that is, the order of the words is about the same. The last paragraph of the Exercise in Lesson 4 is made up of questions which probably caused you no more difficulty than the same ideas in statement form would have. Those beginning *Est-ce à celui* . . . ? can be translated literally, "Is it to the one . . . ?" The last question is no problem, . . . *doit-on rapporter tout le mérite* . . . ?—"is one to (should one) give all the credit . . . ?" These two types of questions illustrate roughly half of the question forms of French. In informal writing and in conversation many questions are begun *Est-ce* . . . (Is it . . .) or *Est-ce que* . . . (Is it that . . .).

Questions with a pronoun as subject (*doit-on* . . . ?—is one to, should one . . . ?) simply have the subject after the verb as we do in English, although the French insert a hyphen between it and the verb. Sometimes the formula appears changed when there are also pronouns used as objects of the verb. In a statement, such objects come between the subject and the verb (see p. 7). In a question, with the subject after the verb, any pronoun objects come first, preceding the verb, as in a statement:

Le tient-on pour prouvé . . . ?—Do you consider it (to be)
proved . . . ?; *L'abandonne-t-il . . . ?* *—Does he give it
up . . . ?

Mais à qui revient la gloire . . . ? (But to whom does the
glory belong . . . ?) illustrates a different form of question. Here
the noun subject follows the verb. In English we put "does" before the noun subject, as we do before a pronoun subject ("does
he"), but since French forms questions without any similar
auxiliary, they sometimes give difficulty. There is a general rule
which states that in questions beginning with an interrogative
word, the subject may simply follow the verb. (The *mais* and
the *à* do not affect the order.) In many questions beginning with
"where, when, why, what, who, whom," etc., this order holds:
Où va l'homme? (Where is the man going?); *Quand commence
l'expérience?* (When does the experiment begin?). Upon oc-
casion this order of verb-subject might lead to ambiguity. As-
sume the French sentence: *Quel chien voit l'homme?* = What
dog sees the man?, or, What dog does the man see? Either meaning is possible. If the context does not make it obvious which is
correct, the Frenchman will be forced to express the question one
of two ways: (*a*) he may use *est-ce que: Quel chien est-ce que
l'homme voit?* (What dog does the man see?), or (*b*) he may use
a more literary form of question: *Quel chien l'homme voit-il?*
(What dog does the man see?). See paragraph 2 of the Exercise—
ces deux caractères . . . sont-ils toujours simultanés? (Are these
two characteristics . . . always simultaneous?), and *Les concentrés de dégrossissage nécessitent-ils un rebroyage?* (Do the

---

* *Il l'abandonne,* in the statement form. What is the meaning of the *-t-* in
the question form *l'abandonne-t-il?* Note that *il y a* in the Exercise below,
5th paragraph becomes *y a-t-il.* Here is the explanation: The *-t-* is inserted
between verb and a following subject pronoun *il, elle,* or *on,* i.e., in inverted
word order, whenever the verb itself does not already end in a *-t* or *-d-.*
Fait-il? (Has he?), *rend-il?* (does he return?) need no extra *-t-.* But *abandonne* and *a* must have a *t*-sound before the 3rd person singular subject
(*-t-il, -t-elle, -t-on*).

rough-ground concentrates need regrinding?) Whenever the subject of a question is a noun, the French may use the latter construction, which is surprising to us in that it differs so much from English usage. Not that such questions are impossible in English. They are possible and even fairly frequent, but they are generally considered "substandard English."

In French, on the contrary, they represent a thoroughly elegant usage. In *Les concentrés . . . nécessitent-ils . . . ?* the question could have been stated in other ways, *Est-ce que les concentrés nécessitent . . . ?*, for instance. But where the subject of the question is a noun and there are also noun objects, the order (1) noun subject, (2) verb, (3) subject pronoun, (4) noun objects, will nearly always be used in written French. *L'homme dans la rue connaît-il l'amour?* could scarcely be written in any other form. In spoken or informal writing *Est-ce que* might be used, but such a rhetorical question practically forces one to adopt the literary turn of phrase.

INVERTED WORD ORDER

When the subject of a sentence, or of a clause, follows the verb, the order is said to be inverted. Many questions have inverted word order, as already mentioned. There is another common construction in which the subject follows the verb in French. In any subordinate clause beginning with *que,* and less commonly with *où* and other subordinate conjunctions or relative pronouns, the subject may follow the verb, provided it is clear to the reader that the subject, in its position after the verb, really is the subject and not an object. When the clause is introduced by *que,* this is perfectly clear; for *que* can never be the subject of a verb. In the last sentence of the Exercise at the end of this lesson there is a somewhat involved example with *que: que permettent de déceler . . . l'approche ou la présence . . .* The subject is the two nouns after the verb. Hence the plural verb.

The translator must be on his guard against the temptation to find a subject ahead of the verb in such constructions. *Que* can never be a subject.

One other rare type of inversion is found in another literary construction. An example occurs in the Exercise in Lesson 4, paragraph 3. *Sans doute évoluera-t-elle.* After a few adverbial expressions like *sans doute* (no doubt), *peut-être* (perhaps), and conjunctions such as *aussi* (so, therefore), inversion will be found. It should cause no trouble as it is not followed by a question mark.

ARTICLES

Articles are little words which are used to define the applications of a noun, to make it definite, or to make it indefinite. They come before any adjectives which modify the noun and even before adverbs modifying the adjectives. Thus far the use of articles in French is like that in English, but when one turns to specific articles and what they express, divergences crop up.

First, the cases where the two languages are alike:

1. The indefinite article "a" ("an" before vowels) shows that the speaker is referring to no particular member of a class but just any representative of it, "a tree, a reason." This idea is expressed in French by *un* before masculine nouns and *une***** before feminine nouns, *un arbre* (a tree), *une raison* (a reason).

2. The definite article "the" designates *the* object or idea in question with the maximum of definiteness possible in the language. Compare "the beaker," where it must be previously under-

---

* Every object or concept, hence every noun, is either masculine or feminine. Articles and other types of noun modifiers usually have different forms according to whether they refer to a masculine or a feminine noun; for the feminine, -*e* is normally added to the masculine. If the masculine ends in -*e*, there is no change. In the plural the feminine -*e* comes before the -*s* of the plural; so the masculine plural ends in -*s*, the feminine in -*es*. There are a few irregular feminines and plurals. (See Lesson 11.)

stood which beaker is involved, with "a beaker," where no particular beaker is meant.

The definite article "the" is translated in French by a word which has many possible forms. They vary according to the word they modify as follows:

French Words for "the"

le   before a singular masculine noun beginning with a consonant: *le fer* (the iron)

la   before a singular feminine noun beginning with a consonant: *la vapeur* (the steam, vapor)

l'   before a singular noun, masculine or feminine, beginning with a vowel: *l'homme* (the man); *l'azote* (the nitrogen)

les before all plural nouns, masculine or feminine, beginning with consonant or vowel: *les fers, les vapeurs, les hommes,* etc.

Unfortunately, there is a further complication in the forms of the French word for "the." Two prepositions *à* and *de* elide with some of the forms given above to make one word as follows:

à + le > au	*au fer* (to the iron)
à + les > aux	*aux fers* (to the irons)
de + le > du	*du fer* (of the iron)
de + les > des	*des fers* (of the irons)

à and *de* do not elide with the other forms of the article, *la* and *l'*. One finds *à la vapeur* (to the steam) or *de l'azote* (of the nitrogen), for example.

Now, in French there are two more articles. These differ in usage from English articles.

3. There is a "partitive" article in French. The name is not illuminating, but no other name would be more so because the concept is unknown to those of us who speak only English. In a way the partitive is similar to the concept expressed by the in-

definite article, but whereas "a" (*un*) can only be used of things which are quantized, the partitive expresses an indefinite amount of something like water, for example. We say "Add water until the boiling stops" but we cannot say "Add a water." In the English "Add water," no article is used before water. The water is just part of all water; the idea is called "partitive." In French an article called the partitive article is used in the singular to express this idea of indefinite amount. *Ajoutez du vin.* (Add wine.) In the plural the French partitive article is used to express an indefinite number of countable things, *des arbres* (trees).

The partitive article is made up of the preposition *de* (of) plus the proper form of *le* to agree with the noun modified. This is a second use of *le*. The forms of the partitive article follow:

singular
- *du* before a masculine singular noun beginning with a consonant: *du fer* (iron)
- *de la* before a feminine singular noun beginning with a consonant: *de la lumière* (light)
- *de l'* before all singular nouns beginning with a vowel: *de l'iode* (iodine)

plural   *des* before all plural nouns: *des mots* (words)

It may occur to *some* readers that we have a word in English which expresses the partitive idea. The word is "some" but it is only partitive in *some* of its uses, the unemphatic ones.

In the above paragraph "*some*" was not used in the partitive sense. In both sentences it had the meaning of "a few." In speaking we mark the difference between that use of "some" and its partitive use by a difference in emphasis. We prolong or stress the "some" which means "a few" or "a little." The other, partitive use of "some" is synonymous with the absence of any word or article. We never stress this "some": I'll take some coffee = I'll take coffee.

In American English we express the partitive more often by the absence of a word than by the unaccented "some." In the negative we express the partitive by "not any, no, none" (I don't want any coffee), or by a negative verb and no adjective (I don't want coffee). The French make the partitive negative by making the verb negative in their usual way, but after a negative the partitive article changes, dropping the form of *le* out of the *de* + *le*, leaving only *de*.

> Il prend *de l'eau* = It takes water.
> Il ne prend *pas d'eau* = It does not take water, or
>   It takes no water.

4. The last use of the article in French is easier to handle for an American than the partitive. Here again we are dealing with forms of *le*, as in the definite article. The identical forms express another idea which is usually called the "general" sense. Take a statement like "Water freezes at 32° F." Leaving aside questions as to the accuracy of the statement, note the absence of any article before "water." Here we are not dealing with the partitive idea, which would also be expressed by absence of any article in English. In "water freezes" we mean water in general, practically all water. This general sense of the thing or concept is expressed by the use of *le* in its correct form to agree with the noun. In English it is translated by the absence of any word, just as the partitive would be: *L'eau gèle à 0° C* (Water freezes at 0° C).

SUMMARY OF ARTICLES

When *le, la, l', or les* is found before a noun, either the definite article is involved and it is translated by "the," or the general sense is involved and no article is needed in English. *Un, une* are translated "a, an." *De*, plus a form of *le*, may be the partitive and then no word is needed in English, though the unstressed "some" may be used.

Once the partitive use of *de* + *le* is clearly in mind, it may be safe to mention the unfortunate fact that *de* plus forms of *le* may not be the partitive at all, in any particular case, but may be *de* (of) plus the definite article *le* (the); *du fer* may mean "iron"; it may mean "of the iron." Let your context be your guide.

SAMPLE SENTENCES

1. Comme le montrent leurs formules de structure, le remplacement d'une de ces molécules par l'autre fournit un autre exemple de mutation chimique.

2. Dans le vol nuptial des fourmis ailées, interviendrait aussi un phototropisme intense.

3. Aussi presque personne ne tente-t-il de construire une théorie qui rende compte de tous les phénomènes observés.

4. Qu'est-ce qu'un mouvement d'onde?

5. Comment peut-on l'expliquer et comment confirme-t-il l'existence des couches électro-aériennes?

6. Ce qui importe surtout, c'est que l'or, ainsi que le reconnaissait encore récemment l'*Economist,* cesse d'être la mesure internationale des monnaies.

7. Mais n'en est-il pas ainsi de toute oeuvre, si imparfaite soit-elle, où entre une part de création?

8. Que répondre à celui qui contestera l'existence de l'âme ainsi définie?

9. L'étude radiocristallographique des hydrure et deutérure de lanthane permet de rapprocher ces variations de celles que présente la microstructure des composés étudiés.

10. Nous avons défini l'intégrale telle que, pratiquement, la conçoit le physico-chimiste.

EXERCISE

Toute laverie de flotation doit être munie d'un laboratoire, non seulement pour le contrôle des teneurs des minerais toutvenant, des concentrés et des stériles, et pour les déterminations de pH et les essais de réactifs, d'eaux, mais aussi pour l'étude des modifications de traitement qui peuvent se présenter par suite de changement dans la nature des minerais traités, et les essais de tamisage (screen analyses) afin de déterminer le meilleur degré ou mesh de broyage pour obtenir des concentrés à haute teneur et avec les meilleurs rendements.

En outre, les laboratoires doivent être munis de microscopes et d'appareils pour la préparation de plaques minces ou de plaques polies afin de préciser la nature des minerais qu'on doit faire flotter. Le microscope permet de répondre aux questions suivantes:

Les concentrés de dégrossissage nécessitent-ils un rebroyage?

Quelle est la nature des pertes de certains minéraux ou métaux?

Y a-t-il des associations privilégiées de certains minéraux?

Quel est le caractère des impuretés que l'on trouve dans les concentrés et est-il désirable de les rejeter?

Dans quel minéral particulier se trouvent les métaux précieux? Peut-on recueillir certains minéraux en petite quantité dans le minerai dont on ne tenait pas compte, mais que la concentration par flotation permet d'obtenir économiquement?

Quels sont les minéraux secondaires que permettent de déceler dans une mine l'approche ou la présence d'un minéral déterminé?—A.-M. GAUDIN, "Le Contrôle du flottage au microscope," *Congrès International des Mines, de la Métallurgie,* etc., Paris, October 1935, pp. 279–284.

Pronouns

The pronouns in French are most easily understood if divided into six classes according to their function: (*A*) those *used with a verb*, as its subject or one of its objects, like "he, him, you"; (*B*) *emphatic pronouns*, used as object of a preposition or in other positions where they are stressed—in a few cases these may also be used as subject or object of a verb; (*C*) *relative pronouns* which introduce a clause, like "who, whom, which," etc.; (*D*) *demonstrative pronouns*, like "this one, these, those"; (*E*) *possessive pronouns* like "its (own)" in *chacun prend le sien* = "each one takes its own"; and (*F*) *interrogative pronouns*. In this lesson only the first three classes of pronouns will be taken up. The next two will be found in Lesson 7, and the interrogative pronouns in Lesson 9.

A. PRONOUNS USED WITH VERB

Table 9 shows the forms of subject and object pronouns in French with their translations. *Nous* (we, us) and *vous* (you) are easy to recognize; for they do not change in their different uses. This uniformity has a drawback for the translator. He has only the position in the sentence and the context to guide him as to the meaning. *Il nous montre . . .* = "It shows us . . ."; *nous nous demandons . . .* = "we ask ourselves" or "each other," or "we wonder." Note also the numerous meanings of *se.*

Two small words that cause a disproportionate amount of trouble to the translator are *y* and *en.* They are given under "Indirect Object, 3rd person singular and plural," but there is some question whether they may correctly be considered as "indirect" objects. They often correspond in English to a preposition with its object pronoun: "to it, of it," or to an adverbial expression: "there, from there." In French *y* and *en* are used grammatically as object pronouns, however their translations may appear in English. Perhaps *en* should be called the partitive object pronoun, yet it replaces not only the partitive "some" or "any" but also the preposition *de* plus any third person pronoun object.

The uses of *y* and *en* may be summarized as follows:

y = *à* + pronoun *le, la,* or *les* = "to it, to them, there," etc.
en = *de* + pronoun *le, la,* or *les* = "some, any, there," or any of the meanings of *de* plus any of the meanings of *le, la* or *les:* "to it, of them, from there," etc.

Examples

Il y ajoute cinq gouttes = he adds five drops (to it, to them)
Il en ajoute cinq = he adds five (of them)
Il y va = he goes there
Il en a trois = he has three (of them)
Il y en a = there are some (of them)
Il y en a trois = there are three (of them)
Il en vient = he comes from there
Nous en sommes à chercher l'explication de ce phénomène = we are looking for the explanation of this phenomenon. (Here *en* means "in the matter in question" and is best omitted in translation.)

TABLE 9. PRONOUNS USED WITH VERB

PERSON		SUBJECT	DIRECT OBJECT	INDIRECT OBJECT [1]	REFLEXIVE AND RECIPROCAL, DIRECT OR INDIRECT OBJECT
1st per.	sing.	je—I	me—me	me—me	me—myself
	plural	nous—we	nous—us	nous—us	nous—ourselves, each other
2nd	sing. or pl.	vous—you	vous—you	vous—you	vous—yourself, yourselves, each other
3rd	sing. masc.	il—he, it	le—him, it	lui—him, her, it	se—himself, herself,
	sing. fem.	elle—she, it	la—her, it	y—it, there	itself, oneself,
				en—of it, some, any	themselves, each
	indefinite	on—one, you, they	vous—one, you	vous—one, you	other
	pl. masc.	ils—they		leur—them	
	pl. fem.	elles—they	les—them	y—them, there	
				en—of them, some, any	

---

[1] The English indirect object is often accompanied by "to" or "for": *Il me la fait*—"He does it to me," or "He does it for me." The French almost never uses a preposition but indicates the indirect object by the form and position of the pronoun. Likewise the reflexives and reciprocals are frequently identifiable only by their context and position.

B. EMPHATIC PRONOUNS

During the development of French from Latin, sounds behaved differently according to whether they were accented (pronounced strongly) or unaccented (passed over lightly). All the pronouns under (A) *Pronouns used with verb* are of the latter type. They developed from Latin forms where the accent, if any, was on the verb, the subject and object pronouns being unaccented.

The emphatic pronouns are different in form because they have come from Latin accented pronouns. As object of a preposition, for instance, only the emphatic form is found. When the subject of the verb is stressed, the emphatic form has to be used. In rare cases (i.e., in an affirmative command) where pronoun objects follow the verb instead of preceding it, the last object pronoun would be expected to be the stressed form, since an accent always falls on the last of a group of words involving a verb, but here logic breaks down and the French of today use a mixture of forms. The first and second persons have the emphatic forms while the third person pronoun objects have the unstressed forms: *le, la, les, lui, leur*.

The emphatic pronoun forms are compared with the unstressed forms in the following table:

TABLE 10. COMPARISON OF PRONOUN FORMS

FRENCH EMPHATIC	ENGLISH EQUIVALENT	FRENCH UNEMPHATIC	
subj. or *obj.*		*subj.*	*obj.*
moi	I, me, to me	je	me
lui (masc.)	he, him, to him, it, to it	il	le, lui
elle (fem.)	she, her, to her, it, to it	elle	la, lui
nous	we, us, to us	nous	nous
vous	you, to you	vous	vous
eux (masc.)	they, them, to them	ils	les, leur
elles (fem.)	they, them, to them	elles	les, leur

Examples

    Avec eux—with them
    Sans elles—without them
    Lui étudie la physique, elle les mathématiques—He studies
      physics, she (studies) math.
    Ouvrez-les-moi—Open them to me, or, Open them for me.

The emphatic pronouns may be used in addition to the un-emphatic forms. *Eux, ils sont en retard!*—*They* are late! *Il le leur a dit à eux!*—He told *them!*, or, He told it to *them!*

Technical French contains few emphatic pronouns. They are included here so that one of their rare appearances will not take you by surprise.

C. RELATIVE PRONOUNS

With the relatives we come to an important type of pronoun. For the record let us recall that the relative pronoun relates, or grammatically connects, a subordinate clause to the noun or pronoun which it modifies. In "the man *who* . . . ; the thing *which* . . . ; the reason *that* . . . ; the one to *whom* . . .", the italicized words are relative pronouns.

In French the relatives may vary in form to agree with the thing or concept to which they refer, their antecedent. One type has masculine, feminine, singular, and plural forms like the article. When a relative is the object of a preposition, as in the last example above, its form may also depend on whether the antecedent is a person or a thing. Lastly, relatives may change according to whether they are subject or object of the verb in the clause which they introduce.

In the following paragraphs the relatives are taken up one by one:

Qui may be the subject of the verb in its clause (*l'appareil qui est* . . . the apparatus which is . . .); it does not agree with its antecedent. *Qui* is translated "who, which, that."

Que is object of the verb in its clause (*l'appareil qu'on voit*—the apparatus which you see; *le nom que je donne*—the name I give). *Que* is translated "who, whom, which, that." *Que* does not agree with its antecedent.

Qui may also be object of a preposition if it refers to a person (*l'homme de qui vous parlez*—The man of whom you are speaking); there is no agreement with the antecedent. Here, *qui* is translated "whom, who."

Lequel agrees in both of its parts with the word to which it refers; *lequel,* m. sing.; *laquelle,* f. sing.; *lesquels,* m. pl.; *lesquelles,* f. pl. But *lequel* does not change in form according to whether it is subject or object of the verb, or object of a preposition. *Lequel* may have any of the uses of *qui* or *que,* but it or *dont* (see below) must be used as the object of a preposition if the word referred to is not a person: *Le chien duquel vous parlez*—"The dog of which you are speaking." Notice *duquel,* in which the preposition *de* joins the *le* of *lequel* to give *duquel.* The first part of *lequel* is felt to be the article. *De* and *à* combine with it to give all the usual contractions: *duquel, desquels, desquelles* but *de laquelle* (= of whom, of which, whose); *auquel, auxquels, auxquelles,* but *à laquelle* (= to whom, to which).

Dont is a special relative pronoun form which may take the place either of *duquel* or of *de qui.* It may refer either to persons or things and has the meanings: "of whom, of which, whose"; *L'homme dont je parle*—The man of whom I am speaking; *Le principe dont je parle*—The principle of which I am speaking; . . . *cet ouvrage, dont je ne doute pas qu'il éveille l'intérêt du public*— . . . this work which I do not doubt will awaken the interest of the public; *Une loi dont les exceptions sont nombreuses*—A law whose exceptions are numerous, or, A law the exceptions to which are numerous.

Both *qui* and *que* may be used in conjunction with *ce* to express "that which," or "what." Likewise *ce dont,* "that of which."

Ce qui est essentiel—what is essential, that which is essential

Tout ce que vous voulez—anything you wish, whatever you wish (lit. all that you wish)

Ce dont il s'agit—what is involved, what it is a question of

TABLE 11. SUMMARY OF RELATIVE PRONOUNS

(With Verbs)

REFERRING TO	SUBJECT OF VERB	DIRECT OBJECT OF VERB
People or things	qui or lequel[1] (who, which, that)	que or lequel (who, whom, which, that)

(With Prepositions)

REFERRING TO	OBJECT OF PREP. À	OBJECT OF PREP. DE	OBJECT OF OTHER PREPS.
People	à qui or auquel (to whom, who)	de qui, duquel, dont (of whom, whose)	qui (whom, who)
Things	auquel (to which)	duquel, dont (of which, whose)	lequel (which)

Note: This lesson brings up at least three of the points which perennially cause difficulty for American students of French. These are *y*, *en*, and *que*. Experience with numerous occurrences of these will make them clear. The inverted word order after *que*, already mentioned on p. 21, is a trap even for fairly experienced readers who forget that *que* never can be the subject of a verb. *Que* can be an interrogative pronoun (= what); it can be an adverb (= than); but the subject of the verb it introduces must be some other word in the clause.

---

[1] Throughout this table *lequel* stands for the various forms which this word may take to agree with the word it refers to.

Note also that only the meanings "to" for *à* and "of" for *de* are used as examples, but remember that each of these prepositions has numerous other meanings: *à* = "to, at, in, by, with," etc.; *de* = "of, from, with," etc.

SAMPLE SENTENCES

1. L'analyse chimique *nous* a montré qu'il y avait déjà une réduction partielle d'ions Mn^{4+} en ions Mn^{2+}.

2. *On* sait que, si ce problème est possible, *il l'*est d'une infinité de manières.

3. *Il y* avait aussi une catégorie intermédiaire des fonctions, celles *qui* étaient représentées à l'aide de plusieurs arcs de courbes géométriques; *on les* considérait plus volontiers comme formées de parties de fonctions.

4. Et cet or, *nous l'*avons dit, restait stérile à Fort Knox.

5. Au mois d'avril 1948 *il y en* avait 17 millions 200 mille.

6. Depuis la fin de l'année dernière, *il* n'est plus question que de crise; *on en* parla d'abord en termes voilés, pour arriver maintenant à *le* faire ouvertement.

7. Les difficultés de Wall Street paraissent marquer l'origine de la dépression; ce qui ne signifie pas qu'*elles en* soient la cause.

8. Remarquons ici que, d'après les postulats sur les forces, sur *lesquels* est basée la mécanique de milieux continus, la pression ne peut subir des sauts brusques.

9. Cauchy énonce d'une manière très précise la définition *dont* on vient de voir deux applications. Pour *lui*, si une fonction $F(x)$ est continue dans un intervalle (a, b), au voisinage *duquel* $F(x)$ est bornée, on peut définir l'intégrale de $F(x)$ dans (a, b).

10. L'application la plus importante qu'*il en* ait faite concerne les marées.

EXERCISE

A ces raisons générales s'ajoute une raison particulière liée à la notion d'indiscernabilité. L'hypothèse de l'indiscernabilité peut être interprétée comme un renoncement à l'individualité des corpuscules, ou tout au moins un renoncement à suivre l'individualité des corpuscules, si l'on entend par individualité la mise en évidence de certaines propriétés intrinsèques appartenant d'une façon permanente à un être, à une entité, à une unité, en somme à un individu. Si notre individu ne possède aucune marque distinctive, nous ne pourrons conserver son individualité que si nous pouvons le suivre et nous la perdons sitôt que des échanges d'individus de même type se font sans qu'il nous soit possible d'en avoir des traces. Or si nous admettons l'indiscernabilité des corpuscules, nous admettons par là l'existence d'échanges dont nous ne pouvons nous rendre compte par aucun moyen. M. Langevin a insisté sur l'intérêt qu'il y aurait à édifier les théories atomiques actuelles en partant de ce renoncement à l'individualité des corpuscules, c'est-à-dire en adoptant l'indiscernabilité des corpuscules de même espèce comme principe fondamental. Il espérait qu'en suivant cette méthode on pourrait rétablir le déterminisme, le renoncement à l'individualité étant un abandon suffisant des notions classiques sans qu'il soit nécessaire d'abandonner aussi le déterminisme (en mécanique ondulatoire on renonce au déterminisme en premier lieu et ceci entraîne l'indiscernabilité d'après le théorème). Un certain nombre de raisons laissaient supposer que le renoncement à l'individualité suffirait, mais Mlle. Février adoptant cette attitude étudia les conséquences de l'indiscernabilité; le résultat de son travail fut d'établir que l'indiscernabilité entraîne l'indéterminisme.—J.-L. DESTOUCHES, *Corpuscules et systèmes de corpuscules,* Paris, Hermann et Cie., 1948.

Pronouns (Continued)

The fourth and fifth categories of pronouns are considered in this lesson, (D) demonstratives and (E) possessives. They are taken up along with their corresponding adjectives because both forms and uses show an interrelationship which makes them easier to understand and remember when they are studied at the same time.

D. DEMONSTRATIVE ADJECTIVES AND PRONOUNS

In English the demonstratives may be used either as adjectives or as pronouns; "this, that, these, those" are adjectives when used with a noun (this report, etc.) or pronouns when used without a noun (with this, this is good, etc.). The French demonstrative pronoun is a modified form of the demonstrative adjective. Both have masculine, feminine, singular, and plural forms. The adjective agrees with the noun it modifies. The pronoun agrees with its antecedent, except for the so-called indefinite pronouns which refer to a whole idea rather than a single noun or pronoun. See Tables 12 and 13 for forms and examples.

The French demonstrative adjective and pronoun do not distinguish two degrees of nearness to the speaker as the English "this" and "that" do. In French there is one adjective *ce* (in its several forms to agree with the noun), meaning "this, that, these, or those" and one pronoun *celui* (in its various forms to agree

TABLE 12. DEMONSTRATIVE ADJECTIVES

FRENCH	ENGLISH	EXAMPLE
m. sing. ce (cet[1])	this, that	ce principe—this, that principle; cet[1] élément—this, that element
ce (cet[1]) . . . -ci	this, the latter	ce principe-ci—this principle, the latter principle
ce (cet[1]) . . . -là	that, the former	ce principe-là—that principle, the former principle
f. sing. cette	this, that	cette analogie—this, that analogy
cette . . . -ci	this, the latter	cette analogie-ci — this analogy, the latter analogy
cette . . . -là	that, the former	cette analogie-là — that analogy, the former analogy
m. and f. pl. ces	these, those	ces principes (analogies)—these, those principles (analogies)
ces . . . -ci	these, the latter	ces principes-ci (analogies-ci) — these principles (analogies), the latter principles (analogies)
ces . . . -là	those, the former	ces principes-là (analogies-là) — those principles (analogies), the former principles (analogies)

---

[1] *Cet* is used before all masculine singular nouns or adjectives beginning with a vowel sound; *ce* is used before consonants and before the so-called aspirate h.

with its antecedent), conveying one of the meanings "this, that, these, or those." In translation therefore, the forms of *ce* and *celui* will have to become "this, that, these, or those" according to the English context.

The French can, if they wish, make the distinction between near-at-hand or far-away which we cannot help making. Two short particles -*ci* (from *ici* = here) and -*là* (= there) are used to add this idea to the basic demonstratives. In the case of the adjective *ce*, -*ci* or -*là* is added to the noun modified by *ce: ce principe* = this, or, that principle; but *ce principe-ci* = this principle; and *ce principe-là* = that principle. With the pronoun *celui*, -*ci*, or -*là* is added directly, giving *celui-ci* (this one) and *celui-là* (that one).

TABLE 13. DEMONSTRATIVE PRONOUNS

FRENCH	ENGLISH	EXAMPLE
m. sing. celui f. " celle	he she that, the one	celui qui—he who, the one which celle qui—she who, the one which celui de Jean—that of John, John's celui que—the one which
m. sing. celui-ci f. " celle-ci m. " celui-là f. " celle-là	this one, the latter that one, the former	celui-ci est brun; celui-là bleu—the former is blue, the latter brown
m. pl. ceux f. " celles	those, they	ceux qui—those who, those which celles de Jean—those of John, John's
m. pl. ceux-ci f. " celles-ci m. pl. ceux-là f. " celles-là	these, the latter those, the former	celles-ci sont jaunes, celles-là sont rouges—the former are red, the latter are yellow

The particles -*ci* and -*là* have another use; they distinguish "the former" from "the latter"; *ce principe-ci* = the latter principle; *ce principe-là* = the former. Note that, while English customarily mentions first the former and then the latter, French invariably treats the ideas in the reverse order, mentioning the latter first, then the former. The translator will have to reverse the order so that normal English will come out: *celui-ci est brun; celui-là, bleu* = the former is blue; the latter, brown.

The indefinite demonstrative pronouns are shown with examples in Table 14. They are *ce, ceci,* and *cela.* Here -*ci* and -*la* are added to the adjective *ce.*

TABLE 14. INDEFINITE DEMONSTRATIVE PRONOUNS

FRENCH	ENGLISH	EXAMPLE
ce	this, that, it, etc.	ce sont les résultats—it is (those are) the results c'est lui—it is he, she, it ce que je constate—that which (= what) I find c'est à voir—that, this, it remains to be seen
ceci	this	ceci est un modèle de . . .—this is a model of . . .
cela	that	il est fait pour cela—it, he is made for that

E. POSSESSIVE ADJECTIVES AND PRONOUNS

Now we come to a situation which is less complicated than the demonstratives. The possessive adjectives are words like "my, his, your," etc., used with a noun. The possessive pronouns are "mine, his, yours," etc., used to refer to something already mentioned. In "Will you take your car or shall I take mine?" "your" is an adjective; "mine" is a pronoun.

Both possessive adjectives and pronouns have differing forms for masculine and feminine, singular and plural; and the French departs fundamentally from English at this point. The English adjectives "his" and "her" are respectively masculine and feminine to agree with the person to whom they refer: "The man and *his* wife; the woman and *her* husband." To us this seems logical.

To the French a different type of agreement is logical. The French possessive adjectives, like their other adjectives, agree with the word modified, not with the possessor: *l'homme et sa femme; la femme et son mari. Sa* is feminine because it modifies *femme*, although it means "his"; *son* is masculine, although it means "her."

In the meaning of French possessive adjectives the situation is analogous to that of the demonstratives where *ce* = "this" or "that." The possessive adjective *son*, in its various forms, means either "his, her," or "its." It is only by adding a prepositional phrase after the noun (*à lui, à elle*, etc.) that the French can distinguish "his" from "her," just as *-ci* and *-là* are used with the demonstratives to distinguish "this" and "that." So, *son enfant* = his child, or, her child. But if a distinction is necessary, that is, if the presence of two possible antecedents of different genders for *son* makes it necessary to distinguish, then "his child" = *son enfant à lui;* "her child" = *son enfant à elle*. In the plural English cannot distinguish masculine from feminine possessors. The French can, by the same mechanism used in the singular: *leurs amis* = their friends; *leurs amis à eux* = their friends (masc. possessors); *leurs amis à elles* = their friends (fem. possessors).

The possessive pronouns are parallel in construction to the possessive adjectives. The agreement is with the antecedent rather than with the possessor. See examples in Table 16. If it is desired to distinguish between masculine and feminine possessors, the same device is used as with adjectives, but the *à lui, à elle, à eux*, etc., follow the pronoun directly. The analogy with the demonstrative pronouns is complete: *le sien* = his, hers, its, or, one's. But *le sien à lui* = his, its: *le sien à elle* = hers, its; *le sien à soi-même* = one's own.

Possessive adjectives and pronouns have been treated together because they are outgrowths of the same original form, just as was the case with demonstrative adjectives and pronouns. The

TABLE 15. POSSESSIVE ADJECTIVES

FRENCH	ENGLISH	NOUN MODIFIED	EXAMPLE
mon ma [1]mon mes	my	m. sing. f. sing. " " m. & f. pl.	mon bras—my arm ma femme—my wife mon[1] amie—my girl friend mes bras, amies—my arms, girl friends
son sa [1]son ses	his, her, its, one's	m. sing. f. sing. " " m. & f. pl.	son bras—his, her, its, one's arms sa main—his, her, its, one's hand son[1] amie—his, her, its, one's girl friend ses bras (mains, amies)—his, her, its, one's arms (hands, girl friends)
notre nos	our	m. & f. sing. m. & f. pl.	notre bras (main, amie)—our arm (hand, girl friend) nos bras (mains, amies)—our arms (hands, girl friends)
votre vos	your	m. & f. sing. m. & f. pl.	votre bras (main, amie)—your arm (hand, girl friend) vos bras (mains, amies)—your arms, (hands, girl friends)
leur leurs	their	m. & f. sing. m. & f. pl.	leur bras (main, amie)—their arm (hand, friend, f.) leurs bras (mains, amies)—their arms (hands, girl friends)

[1] *Mon* and *son* are used before feminine singular nouns beginning with a vowel sound instead of *ma* and *sa*, which are used before consonants and before the so-called aspirate *h* (cf. *ce-cet*).

demonstrative pronouns, for example, are clearly an amalgamation of *ce* and forms of the emphatic pronouns *lui, elle,* etc., giving *celui, celle,* etc. The possessive adjectives and pronouns

TABLE 16. POSSESSIVE PRONOUNS

FRENCH	ENGLISH	ANTECEDENT	EXAMPLE
le mien		m. sing.	ce vin est le mien—this wine is mine
la mienne		f. sing.	cette bière est la mienne—this beer is mine
les miens	mine	m. pl.	ces vins sont les miens—those wines are mine
les miennes		f. pl.	ces bières sont les miennes—those beers are mine
le sien	his, her, its, one's own	m. sing.	ce vin est le sien—this wine is his, hers, its / chacun prend le sien—each one takes his own

(*la sienne, les siens,* and *les siennes* are used like *la mienne,* etc., above)

FRENCH	ENGLISH	ANTECEDENT	EXAMPLE
le nôtre		m. sing.	ce vin est le nôtre—this wine is ours
la nôtre	ours	f. sing.	cette bière est la nôtre—this beer is ours
les nôtres		m. & f. pl.	ces vins (bières) sont les nôtres—these wines (beers) are ours
le vôtre	yours	m. sing.	ce vin est le vôtre—this wine is yours

(*la vôtre, les vôtres* are used like *la nôtre* and *les nôtres*)

FRENCH	ENGLISH	ANTECEDENT	EXAMPLE
le leur	theirs	m. sing.	ce vin est le leur—this wine is theirs

(*la leur, les leurs* are used like *la nôtre* and *les nôtres*) came from the same Latin word, the adjective being the un-accented and the pronoun the accented form. You may find it helpful to observe the parallel between adjective and pronoun: *mon—le mien* (my—mine); *son—le sien* (his—his); *notre—le nôtre* (our—ours); *votre—le vôtre* (your—yours); *leur—le leur* (their—theirs).

SAMPLE SENTENCES

1. Voici *celles que* nous avons déduites dans la série d'essais *dont* il a été question plus haut.

2. Pour que ce point se trouvât sur la courbe, il faudrait déformer *celle-ci.*

3. Le problème est ici étudié directement, et *nous lui* apportons une réponse partielle.

4. Pour *qui* connaît ces lois, *il* n'est pas douteux, que *ce* résultat infirme la première et confirme la seconde.

5. *Ceux-ci* sont considérés comme constituant un continu, de même que l'espace.

6. Le compresseur axial élémentaire se compose, *lui,* d'une rangée d'aubes mobiles.

7. Les trois réactions à considérer durant l'autoxydation sont d'abord la formation de moloxyde, puis l'isomérisation de *celui-ci.*

8. *T* désigne le période, ou durée après *laquelle,* la concentration du moloxyde est réduite à la moitié de la valeur qu'elle avait.

9. Ce sont *celles qui* s'appliquent dans une étude de géologie générale.

EXERCISE

Les avantages de l'analyse par luminescence.—On conçoit sans peine que, puisque chaque substance réagit différemment et réfléchit une fluorescence propre lorsqu'elle est soumise à l'effet

de la lumière de Wood, il y a là une méthode d'analyse extrêmement rapide et pratique.

Une telle méthode présente, entre autres, les remarquables
avantages de la simplicité et de la rapidité.

En toute rigueur, dans des essais scientifiques, il faudrait
établir un spectre de fluorescence. C'est là peut-être la méthode
de demain, mais notre but étant d'envisager et d'étudier les applications pratiques à l'usine dans leur état actuel, nous ne nous
étendrons pas sur les méthodes précises, nécessitant un appareil-
lage délicat et un opérateur exercé. Nous avons en vue le simple
examen visuel et estimatif des couleurs, pouvant être rapporté
à des séries étalon ou à des échantillons de comparaison et, dans
ces conditions, la méthode est extrêmement simple et rapide.

Même dans ces conditions elle peut être sensible. Des traces de
certaines substances suffisent en effet à produire les fluorescences.
C'est ainsi qu'une goutte d'ombelliférone en solution à 1/10.000
suffit pour provoquer, en milieu alcalin, une fluorescence bleue
intense.

Enfin, il est possible d'examiner un corps sans le détériorer,
même par une simple touche et c'est souvent un avantage très
appréciable.

Ses inconvénients.—Si l'analyse par luminescence est sédui-
sante, si elle possède de précieux avantages, elle a aussi ses inconvénients.

Le principal réside dans le fait que, la cause du phénomène
étant imparfaitement connue, des conclusions définitives et des
règles immuables ne peuvent être établies, ce qui fait que la
méthode ne repose pas, en fait, sur des bases très sures.—
M. DÉRIBÉRÉ, *Applications pratiques de la luminescence,* Paris,
Dunod, 1938, p. 26.

Comparisons

A ≈ B

There are numerous ways you can compare two things. One is to equate them: *A* is *as big as B*. Any adjective can take the place of "big" in this expression. The French construction is parallel: *A est aussi grand que B*. With adverbs the situation is the same: "as fast as" = *aussi vite que*.

Oddly enough, when the equation is negative, both our languages can substitute "so" for the first "as": "not as (so) big as" = *pas aussi (si) grand que*. *A n'est pas aussi (si) grand que B* = *A* is not as (so) big as *B; A ne coule pas aussi (si) vite que B* = *A* does not flow as (so) fast as *B*.

A ≳ B

When *A* is bigger or smaller, or more or less than *B*, we may use a special adjective or adverb form ending in -er in the English: "bigger, better, hotter than"; or we may use the word "more": "more important, more instructive, more dense than." The French construction is similar. There are two types of formation. The common way of showing a higher degree is by the use of *plus* (more) before either adjective or adverb. Examples: *plus important que* = more important than; *plus connu que* = better known than.

A few French words cannot use *plus,* just as we cannot say "more good" in English. We have the special word "better" to show a higher degree of "goodness." Certain French adjectives have special forms which are very different words: *bon* (good)—*meilleur que* (better than); *beaucoup* (much)—*plus que* (more than); *petit* (small)—*plus petit que* (smaller than, in size)—*moindre que* (smaller or lesser than, in importance).

Some adverbs in French also have special forms: *bien* (well)—*mieux* (better); peu (little)—*moins* (less); *mal* (badly)—*plus mal* or *pis* (worse).

A ≳ N

When *A* is bigger or smaller than all the others of its class, we use a special construction, called the superlative. One way we form it is to add -est to the adjective or adverb: "biggest, slowest," or "commonest." The rest of our superlatives are formed with the word "most": "most pleasant, most pleasantly," etc.

The French commonly form the superlative of adjectives and adverbs by putting *le plus* before the adjective or adverb: *le plus agréable* = the most pleasant; *le plus agréablement* = the most pleasantly. Note that *plus* = more and most. The difference in French is made by the addition of the article *le* in the superlative. The examples show that *le,* sign of the superlative, agrees as usual when it is used with an adjective, but always remains *le* with an adverb.

Examples of the Superlative

C'est la plus agréable personne!—He (or she) is the pleasantest person!

Ce parfum est plus agréable que l'autre.—This (that) perfume is pleasanter than the other.

Il faut faire cette opération le plus vite possible.—This operation must be performed as fast as possible (lit. the most quickly possible).

In the superlative some French adjectives and adverbs do not use *le plus*. These have special forms: *le meilleur* (the best), *le moins* (the least), etc. The words which have special comparatives generally have special superlatives.

When the superlative adjective follows the noun, an article is used with each: *le travail le plus important*—the most important work. Note the special case of omission of the article in the superlative: *mon meilleur ami*—my best friend, and *mon ami le meilleur*—my best friend. This happens after a possessive adjective.

Table 17 shows the special forms of adjectives and adverbs which, for the most part, are not accompanied by *plus* and *le plus* in comparisons.

TABLE 17. SPECIAL ADJECTIVE AND ADVERB FORMS

(Used in Comparisons)

ADJECTIVES

bon—good	meilleur—better	le meilleur—(the) best
mauvais—bad	pire (fig.) ⎫ worse plus mauvais ⎭	le pire (fig.) ⎫ (the) worst le plus mauvais ⎭
beaucoup—much	plus—more	le plus—(the) most
petit—small	moindre—less (in importance)	le moindre—(the) least
	plus petit—smaller (in size)	le plus petit—(the) smallest

(Example: *C'est le meilleur procédé de tous.*—It is the best process of all.)

ADVERBS

peu—little	moins—less	le moins—(the) least
bien—well	mieux—better	le mieux—(the) best
mal—badly	pis ⎫ worse plus mal ⎭	le pis ⎫ (the) worst le plus mal ⎭

(Example: *Il faut pour le moins essayer.*—One should at least try.)

NEGATIVE EXPRESSIONS

The word "not" in English, with or without a form of "does," makes the sentence negative: "It works"—"it does not work; it did not work; it will not work; it should not work," etc.

In French there is no word to correspond to the "does" but two words are almost invariably used to make a verb negative: *ne* is placed before the verb, or before any object pronouns preceding the verb; and *pas* or one of several other so-called negative words is placed immediately after the verb; in compound tenses right after the auxiliary. For instance: *il ne voyait pas que le gaz ne s'était pas dissipé* (he didn't see that the gas hadn't dissipated).

Some of the more common negative expressions are:

ne . . . pas—not

ne . . . point—not at all

ne . . . guère—hardly

ne . . . jamais—never

ne . . . plus—no more, no longer

ne . . . rien—nothing, not anything

ne . . . pas encore—not yet

ne . . . que—only

ne . . . ni . . . ni—neither . . . nor . . . nor

ne . . . aucun(e)—no, no one, none

ne . . . nul(le)—no, no one, none

ne . . . personne—no one, nobody, not anyone

ne . . . nulle part—nowhere

ne . . . pas . . . non plus—not . . . either

ne . . . plus rien—nothing more, no longer anything

The second half of the negative was originally a noun, in most cases, and had a positive meaning: *ne . . . personne* is "no one" but *une personne* is "a person." So if there is no *ne* in the sentence you could expect to be dealing with the positive. However, in sentences where there is no verb, no *ne* is used; yet the meaning may be clearly negative: *Rien!*—Nothing! *Personne!*—Nobody!, but *Une personne.*—A person. The presence of an article with *pas, point, rien,* and *personne* will show that it is the noun and not a negative exclamation which is involved. On the other hand, *jamais* may mean "ever" or "never." The context will make these cases clear.

Another difficulty in negative sentences sometimes comes from the fact that, while *ne* always remains in its position before the verb, the other half of the negative is movable. It goes with the word it modifies or where the meaning takes it: *pas un chercheur n'y avait jamais pensé*—not one researcher had ever thought of it.

The omission of *ne* in a negative without a verb was mentioned above. Now there are some cases where the *pas* of *ne . . . pas* is omitted with a verb intended to be negative, leaving just the *ne* before the verb. These cases are found only in French of a fairly literary tone, since in conversation the *ne* is rarely heard; so if the *pas* also is dropped the sentence cannot be negative. In literary French, though, four verbs, *cesser, oser, pouvoir,* and *savoir* will be found without *pas* in the negative: *il ne peut*—he cannot; *il ne sait . . .*—he does not know how to . . .

A few other cases of *ne* without *pas* or any other negative word are found in formal French style. In most of these, the *ne* is completely meaningless and must be omitted in translation. It is a relic of an older use where, in a subordinate clause, after certain types of expressions like words for fearing or preventing, after a superlative, or after *sans* (without), etc., an unnecessary *ne* was added: *Je crains qu'il ne vienne*—I am afraid he is coming; *le plus important qu'on n'ait vu*—the most important that has been seen; *sans qu'on ne puisse . . .*—without one's being able . . . (This type of subordinate clause traditionally has its verb in the subjunctive.)

In French the negative expressions are frequently combined, using only one *ne* before the verb of the clause but several of the complementary words *plus, jamais, personne*, etc. Two examples have been given above: *ne . . . plus rien* = nothing more, no longer anything, and *pas un chercheur n'y avait jamais pensé* = not one research man had ever thought of it. Note how the negative applies to one of the complementary words, the others being positive. Other examples are:

Il n'y aura plus jamais personne pour dire . . . = There will never be anyone else to say . . . , there will never again be anyone to say . . .

Il n'y en a guère plus = There is hardly any more.

Il n'y a pas non plus de hausse dans le cas où . . . = There is no rise either in the case in which . . .

Summarizing, we can say that *ne* before the verb is the sign of a negative meaning in the great majority of cases. The *ne* is usually supplemented by *pas* or another word. If there is no verb in the sentence or clause, the second part of the negative expression alone is sufficient. With four verbs (*cesser, oser, pouvoir, savoir*) the *ne* may be used alone.

Other cases of *ne* alone, particularly in subordinate clauses, are not negatives and are omitted in translation.

Just in Passing

Note the descending series: *plusieurs chiffres* (several figures) > *quelque chiffres* (some, a few figures) > *des chiffres* (figures). The absence of a modifier in English gives the same meaning as *des* before a noun in French.

One use of the article may be disconcerting. Once in a while *l'on* is found where you would expect just *on*. This happens only after certain conjunctions: *et l'on, si l'on, que l'on, où l'on* are the most common. It is just an old use of the article in the general sense which is omitted in translation: *et l'on* = and one; *si l'on* = if one; *que l'on* = which one, that one; *où l'on* = where one.

SAMPLE SENTENCES

1. Un des faits *les plus frappants* de la vie américaine des affaires est l'existence d'un nombre considérable d'hommes entreprenants.

2. Je dois vous rappeler le fait que les U.S.A. *n'*ont *pas* eu à souffrir de la destruction de deux guerres.

3. Pour résoudre divers problèmes, nous avons été amenés à doser certains métaux dont nous *ne* disposions *que* de quantités extrêmement faibles.

4. Le jour où cet objectif sera atteint, il *n'*y aura *plus* de problème de la balance des paiements.

5. Un marché à terme *ne* peut donc offrir un champ nouveau à la spéculation.

6. De tels spéculateurs sont *plus nuisibles* qu'utiles.

7. Alors que les biens directs ont une utilité en soi, les autres *n'*en ont une *que* comme rouages du mécanisme de la production et leur valeur *n'*a *plus aucune* signification en dehors de ce mécanisme.

8. On *ne* s'est *guère,* jusqu'ici, occupé de ces courants, sauf en ce qui concerne les cas tout spécial de la circulation générale de l'atmosphère où les inégalités de température *n'*ont d'ailleurs *qu'*une influence secondaire.

9. Mais les procédés d'investigation des courants produits dans une telle nappe sont *bien* difficiles à imaginer.

10. Dans ce cas, il devient possible d'observer les courants dans leurs *moindres* détails.

11. Mais Minnich a montré qu'il *n'*en était *rien* et que le phototropisme *n'*était *pas plus* développé *qu'*à toute autre période.

12. Quant à leur physiologie, nous *n'*en savons à peu près *rien.*

13. J'ai essayé une hypothèse dont la portée soit *aussi générale que* possible.

14. Les verres, les résines, les liquides eux-mêmes ont une structure qui *n'*est *pas aussi* éloignée de la structure cristalline *qu'*on le pensait antérieurement.

15. Ces problèmes qui, pour *n'*être *pas aussi* difficiles à résoudre *que* ceux de structures cristallines, *n'*en sont *pas moins* toujours assez délicats.

16. Les ions *F ne* sauraient former de ponts dans le réseau atomique du verre.

17. Mais la représentation graphique est, à ce point de vue, bien *meilleure.*

18. *Aucune* discontinuité de ce genre *ne* se présente au passage de l'état liquide à l'état vitreux.

EXERCISE

Si nous n'avons pas eu la malchance de nous trouver dans le champ d'action de la bombe atomique, ce que nous avons appris de ses effets suffit à combler notre imagination.

En revanche, nous passons toute notre existence au milieu d'une implacable grêle de rayons cosmiques, particules atomiques en mouvement, dont l'énergie peut être plusieurs milliers de fois plus grande que celle des particules émises par les corps radioactifs.

C'est, d'ailleurs, par la valeur de leur énergie et par leur très grand pouvoir de pénétration, que les rayons cosmiques se distinguent essentiellement des diverses radiations. Par bonheur pour nous, la grêle sous laquelle nous évoluons n'est pas trop drue. Sur la surface de la paume de la main passe en moyenne un rayon cosmique toutes les secondes. Mais cette rareté relative, si elle nous épargne les effets d'une dense propagation, n'est pas sans gêner les chercheurs. Leurs observations sont longues et doivent être multipliées à l'infini pour apporter des précisions infimes.

Depuis qu'en 1910 le physicien suisse Gockel, s'étant élevé en ballon à 4.500 mètres, constata que les décharges de son électroscope s'effectuaient plus rapidement que sur la terre et ne pouvaient plus, en conséquence, provenir de la radioactivité du sol, près de cinq cents chercheurs se sont penchés sur le problème de la nature et de l'origine du rayonnement cosmique.

Au premier rang d'entre eux, se trouvent des savants français tels que MM. Pierre Auger, A. Dauvillier, Leprince-Ringuet qui, malgré les plus grandes difficultés, sont parvenus souvent à dépasser les étrangers.

C'est dans son laboratoire de l'Ecole Polytechnique, où il travaille avec une équipe de tenaces auxiliaires, que nous avons pu joindre M. Louis Leprince-Ringuet, dont les travaux sur les rayons cosmiques (particulièrement les mesures de masses d'une incroyable ténuité) ont atteint la plus large notoriété et qui vient de publier un imposant ouvrage illustré mettant à la portée du public l'ensemble des connaissances actuelles sur la question.—*Lu et Vu*, Vol. III, No. 3, March 1947.

Interrogative Adjectives and Pronouns

The sixth and last category of pronouns, the interrogatives, is taken up in this lesson along with the corresponding adjectives. They were not discussed earlier because of the danger of confusion between the interrogative and the relative pronouns. The two classes are similar in form but different enough in use to cause some trouble.

The interrogative adjectives of English, "which?" and "what?" are translated in French by forms of *quel?*: *quel homme?* (which, what man?), *quelle femme?* (which, what woman?), *quels hommes?* (which, what men?), *quelles femmes?* (which, what women?). Other examples are given in Lesson 5 under *Questions*.

The interrogative pronoun *lequel* means "which?" or "which one?" It always refers to something mentioned in the context. Both parts, *le* and *quel*, agree with the thing referred to, masculine or feminine, singular or plural: *lequel de ces deux minerais contient le minéral précité?*—Which of these two ores contains the above-mentioned mineral? *Cette méthode est celle de laquelle on discute le plus à présent.*—This method is the one which is most under discussion at present. Masculine plural: *lesquels;* feminine plural: *lesquelles.*

In translation no trouble is caused by the fact that the forms of *lequel* may be either interrogative or relative pronouns. "Which" in English serves as both, too. A question mark at the end of the sentence provides an unmistakable cue to the interrogatives in both languages.

F. INDEFINITE INTERROGATIVE PRONOUNS

Now we turn to the words for "who?, what?" as interrogative pronouns, called indefinite because the thing referred to is not given but is questioned.

The forms of the indefinite interrogative pronoun "who?, what?" vary according to whether the thing referred to is (1) a person or (2) a thing, just as in English. Their use as subject or object does not change the form here as it did in the relative *qui.* (For persons, English may change: who?—whom?)

1. Qui *Refers to Persons*

Qui l'a fait?—Who did it?
Qui est-ce qui l'a fait?—Who did it? (lit. Who is it who did it?)
Qui voyez-vous?
Qui est-ce que vous voyez? } Who (whom) do you see?

A qui l'a-t-il présenté?
A qui est-ce qu'il l'a présenté? } { To whom did he present it?
Whom (who) did he present it to? }

2. Que *Refers to Things*

There is no subject form for *que?* = what?, referring to things. Where "what" is the subject in English, the French have to use *Qu'est-ce qui* (see example). Then *qui,* the relative, becomes the subject and *que,* the interrogative, is object.

Qu'est-ce qui l'a fait?—What did it?

Que voyez-vous? ⎫
Qu'est-ce que vous voyez? ⎭ What do you see?

Note the use of *est-ce-que.* This type of question is discussed in Lesson 5.

Quoi *Refers to Things*

Quoi (= what) is another indefinite interrogative. It is used to refer to things questioned, and it is found in only two uses: (1) standing alone as an exclamation or question, (2) as object of a preposition. It is the form which developed from Latin in these emphatic positions, parallel to *que* in the unemphatic positions. The origin and use of these two forms are entirely analogous to those of emphatic and unemphatic pairs of the personal pronouns, *moi* and *me,* etc.

Quoi?, Quoi!—What?, What!

A quoi l'a-t-il su? ⎫
A quoi est-ce qu'il l'a su? ⎭ How (lit. By what) did he know it?

De quoi s'agit-il? ⎫
De quoi est-ce qu'il s'agit? ⎭ What is it about?

SUMMARY OF INTERROGATIVES

Adjectives

Quel (quelle, quels, quelles)?—which, what?

Pronouns (Noun or pronoun referred to is expressed)

Lequel (laquelle, etc.)?—who, whom, which, what?

Indefinite Pronouns (Reference is in question)

REFERENCE TO A PERSON:
qui?—who, whom?

REFERENCE TO A THING:

qu'est-ce qui?—what? (unemphatic
  subject)
que?—what? (unemphatic object)
quoi?—what? (emphatic)

NUMBERS

Numbers are usually given in figures but it is necessary to
recognize them when they are written out, as they may be both
in French and in English.

There are three main types of numbers: (*a*) the cardinal numbers, which serve as labels (number one, room ten) or specify
number (fifty degrees, a hundred dollars); (*b*) the ordinal numbers, which establish an order (first, tenth, etc.). Then there are
(*c*) the decimals and fractions, which are a mixture of the other
two types (two and five hundredths, for example).

(a) Cardinal Numbers

un, une—one
deux—two
trois—three
quatre—four
cinq—five
six—six
sept—seven
huit—eight
neuf—nine
dix—ten
onze—eleven
douze—twelve
treize—thirteen
quatorze—fourteen
quinze—fifteen

seize—sixteen
dix-sept—seventeen
dix-huit—eighteen
dix-neuf—nineteen
vingt—twenty
vingt et un—twenty-one
vingt-deux—twenty-two
vingt-trois—twenty-three
vingt-quatre—twenty-four
vingt-cinq—twenty-five
vingt-six—twenty-six
vingt-sept—twenty-seven
vingt-huit—twenty-eight
vingt-neuf—twenty-nine
trente—thirty

The numbers 31–39, 41–49, etc., are formed like 21–29. Hence if you know the decades and the words for hundred, thousand, million, etc., you can count as high as you wish.

vingt—twenty	quatre-vingt-dix—ninety
trente—thirty	cent—hundred
quarante—forty	mille—thousand
cinquante—fifty	un million—a million (10^6)
soixante—sixty	un billion (milliard)—a billion (10^9)
soixante-dix—seventy	un trillion—a trillion (10^{12})
quatre-vingts—eighty	

Note: The British and German billion and trillion are different: 10^{12} and 10^{15} respectively.

In the French numbering system one can see a survival of the Celtic habit of counting by twenties. Perhaps the Celts used fingers and bare toes. The Roman system of counting by tens is used in English from thirteen up. In French it is used from *dix-sept* (seventeen) up, but the French revert to the Celtic system of counting by twenties from *soixante* (60) to *soixante-dix-neuf* (79) and *quatre-vingts* (80) to *quatre-vingt-dix-neuf* (99).

(b) Ordinal Numbers

The ordinal numbers are based on the cardinal numbers, as in English. We add *-th* to the cardinal numbers from four up. The French add *-ième* to the cardinals from *deux* up: *deuxième* (second), *troisième* (third), *vingt-cinquième* (twenty-fifth), etc. Minor changes occur in forming *cinquième* from *cinq* and *neuvième* from *neuf*.

There is an alternate form for "second." It is *second*, m., *seconde*, f. This and "first," *premier, première,* have different masculine and feminine forms to agree with the noun modified or referred to.

Abbreviations may give some trouble, particularly for "first"

and "second." Following is a list of the first few ordinals and
their abbreviations:

1st	(masc.)	—premier, 1er, 1°
	(fem.)	—première, 1e, 1ère, 1°
2nd	(masc.)	—second, 2^d, 2°
	(fem.)	—seconde, 2e, 2°
	(m. and f.)	—deuxième, 2e, 2°
3rd	(m. and f.)	—troisième, 3e, 3°
4th	(m. and f.)	—quatrième, 4e, 4°

(c) Decimals and Fractions

The decimals offer no problem except in their use of the
comma for the decimal point. Those who know German will
recognize this: $3,5 = 3.5$; 0 g, $5 = 0.5$ g; $2cm^3,3 = 2.3$ cc. Where
we use a comma between thousands, the French use a dot. So
French $12.526,05 = 12,526.05$.

Most of the fractions like one-fifth, three-tenths, etc., are
formed with the cardinal for the numerator and the ordinal for
the denominator as in English: *un cinquième* (1/5), *trois dixièmes*
(3/10), etc. But there are two special words for "half," an adjective *demi,* which agrees with the noun modified: *un demi tour*
(a half turn), *une demie livre* (a half pound); and a noun, *une
moitié* (a half). Special words may be used for "third" and
"quarter," but for higher fractions only the regular ordinals are
used.

$1/2 =$ un demi *m.,* une demie *f.,* une moitié
$1\ 1/2 =$ un et demi *m.,* une et demie *f.*
$1/3 =$ un tiers, un troisième
$2\ 2/3 =$ deux et deux tiers, deux et deux troisièmes
$1/4 =$ un quart, un quatrième
$5\ 3/4 =$ cinq et trois quarts, cinq et trois quatrièmes
$1/5 =$ un cinquième, $1/6$ un sixième, etc.

DEVOIR

Devoir: to owe, be to, have to, probably have, must.

This is undoubtedly the most difficult French verb to translate. It has a literal meaning "to owe" which causes no trouble, but it also has figurative meanings which express two quite different ideas, obligation or probability. These meanings differ from tense to tense as the following examples show:

Past	nous avons dû ajouter	we must have added
	nous dûmes ajouter	we had to add
	nous devions ajouter	we were to add
		we had to add
	nous avions dû ajouter	we had had to add
		we must have added
Present	nous devons ajouter	we are to add
		we have to add
		we must add
Future	nous devrons ajouter	we shall have to add
	nous aurons dû ajouter	we shall have to have added
		we shall probably have added
Conditional	nous devrions ajouter	we should, ought to add
	nous aurions dû ajouter	we should, ought to have added

SAVOIR AND POUVOIR

Savoir and *pouvoir* both mean "to be able," but *savoir* refers to something you can do because you have learned how, whereas *pouvoir* refers to something you are physically able to do.

Savoir: to know, to know how; can, to be able
    il sait le français—he knows French

il sait compter—he knows how to count

il sait lire le français—he knows how to (can, is able to) read French

Pouvoir: can, to be able

on peut voir monter les bulles—the bubbles can be seen rising

il a pu constater—he was able to determine, prove

One More Use of Que

In addition to being a pronoun (which, what?, who?, etc.) and an adverb (as, than), *que* may be a subordinating conjunction. *On dit que . . .* = it is said that . . .

SAMPLE SENTENCES

1. Nous avons *pu* atteindre des quantités d'électricité allant jusqu'à 350 Cb par gramme de bioxyde.

2. La proportion de Mn^{4+} réduite à l'état de Mn^{2+} nous a permis de déterminer la quantité d'électricité qui devrait correspondre à cette réduction.

3. Une autre loi fédérale pose un certain nombre de définitions des conditions de travail qui doivent être appliquées dans l'exécution de contrats, passés par le gouvernement des Etats-Unis.

4. On peut alors effectuer une séparation totale d'un corps.

5. Pour réaliser un dosage exact, on doit donc résoudre un triple problème.

6. Dès le début de ces études, je prévoyais que le fluor décomposerait l'eau quand on pourrait l'isoler.

7. Dans le même ouvrage le même auteur admet qu'il ne pouvait être question d'une démonstration logique de la première loi de Maxwell.

8. L'arrêt de la propagation de l'auréole par le bord du

récipient n'est pas marqué comme on aurait pu s'y attendre, par une discontinuité de l'intensité du courant.

9. Mais cet instinct a dû être singulièrement renforcé par le fait que les richesses sont rares.

10. Les modifications dues à l'état d'angoisse peuvent être ramenées à trois types principaux.

EXERCISE

Les graves événements que la France traverse amènent chacun, individus ou groupements, à envisager avec plus de clairvoyance les devoirs de l'avenir; toutes les volontés sont tendues vers le bien du pays; elles se cherchent pour se coordonner, et de toutes parts, à l'apparition de besoins évidents, les projets naissent et les programmes s'élaborent.

Parmi tous ces problèmes qui dès maintenant se posent, les questions de l'organisation scientifique sont de celles qui préoccupent le plus vivement, je ne dirai pas l'opinion publique, mais la partie de cette opinion qui aperçoit avec clarté le rôle de plus en plus considérable que doit jouer la Science dans la société moderne.

Jusqu'ici, l'effort scientifique en France a été surtout individuel, et l'on ne peut nier que cette forme de travail qui s'adapte singulièrement bien au génie de notre race n'ait donné des résultats de première importance: qu'il nous suffise de rappeler les admirables découvertes de Curie travaillant dans un semblant de laboratoire et avec des moyens matériels manifestement insuffisants; celles de Fresnel, démêlant les lois les plus fines de l'Optique avec des instruments réduits à quelques miroirs, quelques lentilles et quelques morceaux de liège; celles d'Ampère faisant à grand'-peine construire les appareils nécessaires à l'établissement de ses théories sur l'Electromagnétisme.

Il y a dans ces recherches une grande part de hasard: on ne peut imposer à personne l'obligation de faire une grande découverte. Dans les laboratoires subventionnés par l'Etat qui poursuivent des recherches de cet ordre, la seule garantie réside dans le choix des hommes qui sont placés à leur tête; c'est à cette catégorie qu'appartiennent entre autres les laboratoires scientifiques universitaires.—HENRI LAUGIER.

Idiomatic Expressions

In this lesson there are numerous words and expressions which often cause trouble to the translator. They seem always to be the same ones, so they are listed here. Learn as many as you can. Until you do, you will find yourself looking them up in the dictionary over and over again. Only the commonest ones are given.

Not all the items here are idiomatic expressions. Some are simply words which look like some English word but are different in meaning (*sensible* = sensitive; ≠ sensible). Others are words which differ in construction from their English counterparts (*de plus en plus* = more and more). Then there are numerous prepositions, adverbs, and conjunctions which merely have to be recognized when met.

Perhaps an arrangement according to parts of speech, which in turn are based on the function of the word in the sentence, will seem less arbitrary than a purely alphabetical one.

NOUNS

expérience, une—an experiment, experience
sensibilité, la—sensitivity, sensibility (≠ sensibleness)

ADJECTIVES

actuel—present ($\neq$ actual)
au point—adjusted, perfected
dit—said, above-mentioned (la dite exception—the above-mentioned exception)
sensible—sensitive, perceptible ($\neq$ sensible)

VERBS

constater—to ascertain, state, verify, record
couler—to flow, leak, sink, cast, scald, etc.
doser—to measure, to determine (proportion of ingredients); ($\neq$ to dose)
réaliser—to fulfill, construct; (rarely: to realize)
rester—to remain ($\neq$ to rest)
consacrer à—to devote to
faire bouillir—to have boil, to make boil, to boil
faire faire un appareil à quelqu'un—to have an apparatus made for (or by) someone
manquer de—to fail to, to just miss (doing something)
porter sur—to bear on
s'agir de—to be a matter (question) of (*Example:* il s'agit de—it is a matter of)
se mettre à—to begin, start, set about
se passer de—to get along without
venir de—to come from
   venir de + infinitive—to have just done something (*Example: Il vient de se refroidir*—It has just cooled)

VERBAL EXPRESSIONS

avoir besoin de—to need (to)
avoir raison—to be right
avoir tort—to be wrong

donner naissance à—to give rise to
faire place à—to give way to
mettre en évidence—to show
mettre en jeu—to put into operation, bring to bear, risk
mettre en oeuvre—to put to work
s'effectuer—to take place
se rendre compte de quelque chose—to take something into account, to realize something
tenir compte de quelque chose—to take something into account
il ne faut pas—one must not, it is necessary not (to); never "it is not necessary" which is *il n'est pas nécessaire*

ADVERBIAL EXPRESSIONS

à la fois—at the same time, both
à part—apart, leaving aside
à peine—hardly, scarcely
à peu près—nearly
à plusieurs reprises—on several occasions
à point—just right
actuellement—at present ($\neq$ actually)
ailleurs—elsewhere
au moins—at least
au plus—at the most
d'abord—first
d'ailleurs—moreover
d'une part . . . d'autre part—on the one hand . . . on the other hand
de même—likewise
de plus—moreover
de plus en plus—more and more

de proche en proche—gradually
dès lors—from then on
du moins—at least
en moyenne—on the average
en outre—besides
ensuite (= puis)—then, next
par contre—on the other hand
puis (= ensuite)—then, next
quand même—all the same, even if
tant . . . (à cause de sa légèreté) qu' (à cause de son prix)—both . . . (because of its lightness) and . . . (because of its price)
tantôt . . . (ceci) . . . tantôt . . . (cela) . . .—now . . . (this) . . . now . . . (that) . . .
tout au moins—at the very least
tout au plus—at the very most

PREPOSITIONS AND PREPOSITIONAL PHRASES

à la suite de—after
à partir de—starting with
à titre de—under the heading of, as
afin de—in order to
au cours de—in the course of, during
au fur et à mesure (de)—during, as, in proportion (to)
au lieu de—in place of
au moyen de—by means of
au sein de—within

d'après—according to
du fait de—from the fact of, because of
en dehors de—outside of, except for
en raison de—by reason of
en vue de—in sight of, with a view to
le long de—along
lors de—at the time of
par suite de—as a result of
quant à—as to, as for

CONJUNCTIONS

à savoir—namely
à mesure que ⎫
alors que   ⎬ whereas
au lieu que   ⎭
afin que—in order that
d'autant plus (moins) que—all the more (less) since, all the more (less) when
d'autant que—since
de sorte que—so that
dès que—as soon as
d'où—whence
du fait que—from the fact that, because
en tant que—as
étant donné que—considering that, given
lorsque—when

quand même—even if, all the same
que—which, what, that, whom, than, as
(Note: *que* can be used in place of repeating any other conjunction. *Example: S'il est désirable et qu'il paraisse possible, on peut . . .*—If it is desirable and if it appears possible, one can . . .)
quoi que—whatever
quoique—although
soit . . . soit—either . . . or
tant que—as long as, as much as
tout en (= en)—while

Most of the compound prepositions end in *de;* many of the
compound conjunctions end in *que.* Compare *afin de* (in order
to)—*afin que* (in order that), *du fait de* (because of the fact of)
—*du fait que* (because of the fact that), etc. The prepositions
introduce nouns, pronouns, and frequently infinitives; the conjunctions always introduce a subordinate clause.

THE USE OF *FAIRE*

Faire with a noun or pronoun object means "to make" or "to
do." *Il fait l'expérience*—He makes the experiment.

Faire with an infinitive as object means "to have" or "to
cause." The infinitive is then passive in meaning. *Faire voir*—to
show (lit., "to cause to be seen"). Both uses may be combined:
faire faire une expérience—to have an experiment done.

CONVENIR

il convient (*de*)—it is suitable, fitting, proper (to), ≠ it is con-
venient

un inconvénient—a disadvantage, drawback, objection, ≠ in-
convenience

SAMPLE SENTENCES

1. *Au fur et à mesure* que l'étude de la chimie s'est dé-
veloppée scientifiquement on a constaté que ce genre de réactions était extrêmement général.

2. Les montages utilisés *tiennent compte* des derniers perfec-
tionnements de la technique électromagnétique.

3. Au cours de recherches sur la décharge en haute fréquence,
j'ai *mis en évidence* un nouvel effet.

4. Le tube à décharge est muni, *d'une part,* de deux électrodes
externes, et, *d'autre part,* de deux électrodes internes.

5. La décharge se présente sous la forme d'une colonne lumineuse de brilliance *à peu près* uniforme.

6. Cette multiplication de déterminations expérimentales lui permettra *à la fois,* de contrôler ses résultats et de préciser l'allure de cette courbe.

7. L'analogie remarquée entre les lois de la mécanique analytique et celles de l'optique géométrique semblait indiquer *qu'il y avait lieu* de construire une théorie synthétique.

8. Les milieux officiels ont commencé par essayer de déguiser le caractère troublant de la conjoncture, en assurant qu'il ne pouvait *s'agir* que d'une agitation momentanée.

9. Planck apercevait la nécessité d'introduire dans la théorie un élément *tout à fait* étranger aux conceptions classiques.

10. Pour *mettre en oeuvre* ces idées directrices, on pouvait s'appuyer sur des considérations tirées de la théorie de la Relativité.

11. Nous voudrions montrer que, *tout en prolongeant* les théories antérieures de l'atome, elle nous a apporté des idées très nouvelles.

12. L'Angleterre *était en mesure de* faire face à cette dette *grâce aux* revenus des ses investissements outre-mer.

13. Mais, *à mesure que,* les sociétés se développaient, la violence individuelle a cédé à la puissance collective.

14. On peut préciser les deux premiers théorèmes qui *viennent* d'être obtenus.

EXERCISE

La préparation des aliments déshydratés est un exemple typique de ce que la nécessité peut imposer aux hommes. C'est aussi une excellente preuve de la rapidité avec laquelle un problème peut être résolu lorsque toutes les données scientifiques qui le conditionnent sont connues et que le travail de mise au point est entrepris en coopération par des practiciens avisés qui savent surmonter un à un tous les obstacles qui se dressent devant les hommes chaque fois qu'ils se décident à mettre debout une nouvelle industrie. Il ne faut pas oublier en effet que les mises au point des données de la science en vue de produire, au sens économique du mot, posent toujours des problèmes nouveaux. Ces problèmes sont à la fois d'ordre scientifique, technique, économique et social.

L'obligation actuelle de déshydrater des aliments est venue, en premier, du besoin de transporter le maximum de vivres dans le minimum d'espace, cela surtout pour les transports maritimes. En second, de supporter la disette en étain employé à la fabrication des boîtes de conserve, après la mainmise du Japon en 1940 sur les gisements de minerai de l'Asie qui fournissaient 70% de l'étain utilisé sur le globe.

La dessication, ou séchage lent des denrées alimentaires, est pratiquée depuis fort longtemps pour conserver les aliments. La déshydration est un procédé de dessication rapide qui s'est développé récemment, en partant de l'industrie de denrées très périssables comme les oeufs et le lait. On sait que tous nos aliments, qu'ils soient d'origine végétale ou animale, renferment une grande quantité d'eau, de 65% à 95%. En enlevant l'eau d'une substance alimentaire, on empêche les phénomènes diastasiques normaux de se produire; on contrarie tellement la vie des microbes qu'ils ne peuvent plus se multiplier. La denrée sèche peut alors se conserver longtemps sans changer d'aspect et en gardant la plus grande partie de sa valeur nutritive.—Louis Bourgoin, *Science sans douleur,* Montréal, La Revue Moderne, 1943.

Plural of Nouns and Adjectives

In this lesson are grouped some remarks about plurals, genders, and spelling peculiarities. These are not things which should cause much trouble to the translator and it is suggested that you simply read through this lesson to see what types of changes occur. This may help you to puzzle out what the masculine singular of a given noun or adjective is so you can look it up in the dictionary. Dictionaries rarely list feminine and plural forms alphabetically.

The plural of most nouns and adjectives in French is formed by adding an unpronounced -s to the singular.

SINGULAR	PLURAL
le coin (the die, corner)	les coins (the dies, corners)
la nouveauté (the novelty)	les nouveautés (the novelties)
grand, m. (big, large)	grands, m. (big, large)
grande, f. (big, large)	grandes, f. (big, large)

If the singular ends in -s, -x, or -z there is no change in the spelling for the plural. (*le bras, les bras*—arm, arms; *vieux*—old, m. sing. and pl.)

The plural of the great majority of French nouns and adjectives sounds like the singular. It is the sound of other associated words like the article or the verb, or the context which tells the hearer whether he is dealing with a singular or a plural.

A few nouns and adjectives have plurals formed "irregularly"; that is, in ways other than those already mentioned. The following examples illustrate most of these cases:

SINGULAR ENDING	PLURAL ENDING	EXAMPLE
-al	-aux	minéral, minéraux = mineral, -s
-ail	-aux	émail, émaux = enamel, -s
-au	-aux	eau, eaux = water, -s
-eu	-eux	feu, feux = fire, -s
-ou	-oux	genou, genoux = knee, -s

Not all singulars with the above endings form their plural as indicated. Some follow the general rule and add *s*: (*final, finals* = final; *bleu, bleus* = blue).

GENDER OF NOUNS

There are some nouns whose gender seems illogical, as where a feminine noun may refer to a man; for instance, *la personne* (the person). On the other hand, a noun may remain masculine for both sexes: *l'auteur*, m. (the author, or authoress). Only with a few nouns do the French simply use whichever gender is logical, as in *un enfant* (a boy baby), *une enfant* (a girl baby).

MASCULINE	FEMININE	EXAMPLE
-eur	-euse	polisseur, polisseuse (polisher)
-ien	-ienne	physicien, physicienne (physicist)
-teur	-trice	acteur, actrice (actor, actress)

The feminine ending *-euse* is used to form a large class of names of machines: *une polisseuse*—a polishing machine; *une laveuse*—a washing machine; *une fraiseuse*—a milling machine, etc.

Sometimes the spelling of a word may remain the same but a change from masculine to feminine changes the meaning: *le livre* (the book), *la livre* (the pound); *le manche* (the handle), *la manche* (the sleeve); *le vapeur* (the steamer), *la vapeur* (the steam, vapor). These are completely different words which happen to be spelled alike.

GENDER OF ADJECTIVES

Unfortunately, some short, common adjectives have complicated ways of forming the feminine. An attempt is made below to divide them into five classes, (*a*) to (*e*).

a. Adjectives with the masculine ending in *-l, -n, -s, -t* may double the final consonant before adding *-e* as: *nul, nulle* (no, null), *bon, bonne* (good), *gros, grosse* (big, bulky), etc.

b. Certain adjectives have a special masculine singular form in *-l*, used before a following word beginning with a vowel. The feminine sounds the same but has the *l* doubled and an *-e* added.

MASCULINE	FEMININE	ENGLISH
beau, bel	belle	fine, beautiful, handsome
fou, fol	folle	mad, crazy
mou, mol	molle	soft
nouveau, nouvel	nouvelle	new
vieux, vieil	vieille	old

A Frenchman would therefore write: *un nouveau principe* (a new principle), *un nouvel élément* (a new element), *une nouvelle idée* (a new idea).

c. All adjectives whose masculine form ends in *-er*, and some in *-et*, change the *e* to *è* and then add *-e* after the *-r* or *-t* to form the feminine: *léger, légère* (light); *complet, complète* (complete).

d. In some adjectives, before *-e* is added to form the feminine, the final consonant of the masculine undergoes changes as follows:

CONSONANT CHANGE   EXAMPLES

$$c > \begin{cases} ch \\ qu \end{cases}$$

blanc—blanche (white)
public—publique (public)

f > v   actif—active (active)
g > gu   long—longue (long)
x > s   fièvreux—fièvreuse (feverish)

The category $x > s$ is very numerous, containing hundreds of adjectives with masculine in *-eux* and feminine in *-euse*.

e. A few adjectives form their feminines in other ways: *doux, douce* (sweet, gentle); *aigu, aiguë* (sharp, acute).

THE SPELLING OF A FEW VERBS

As a general rule the French like to keep the sound of the stem, or part of the verb to which endings are added, the same throughout the various tenses. Verbs which are consistent in this way are called regular. But a verb may be regular in sound and "irregular" in spelling. This happens when French spelling convention requires different letters to show the same sound, because of the letter following; for example, when the consonant at the end of the stem is *c* or *g*. Before *e, i,* and *y, c* and *g* stand respectively for the sounds of "s" and "z" (as in "azure"). Before *a, o,* and *u* they represent hard "k" and "g." So, to maintain the soft sound of the infinitive stem throughout the conjugation, *c* and *g* are changed to *ç* and *ge* whenever they happen to come before an ending beginning with *a, o,* or *u.*

Examples will make this clearer:

MANGER (TO EAT)	COMMENCER (TO BEGIN)
il mange (he eats)	il commence (he begins)
il a mangé (he ate)	il a commencé (he began)
il mangera (he will eat)	il commencera (he will begin)

But

mang*e*ant (eating)	commen*ç*ant (beginning)
il mang*e*ait (he ate)	il commen*ç*ait (he began)
il mang*e*a (he ate)	il commen*ç*a (he began)

In the present tenses, both indicative and subjunctive, and usually also in the future and conditional there is a spelling change in the -e- of verbs ending in -eler or -eter in the infinitive. Here it is actually a change in the sound of this last vowel of the stem which is reflected in the spelling. An example of each of the types of spelling change is given below for the present indicative and the future.

INFINITIVE	PRESENT	FUTURE
accélérer (to accelerate)	il accélère	il accélérera
appeler (to call)	il appelle	il appellera
geler (to freeze)	il gèle	il gèlera
jeter (to throw)	il jette	il jettera
mener (to lead)	il mène	il mènera

One other spelling change in a few verbs is that of *y* to *i* under conditions identical with those for *e* to *è*, etc.; that is, before an ending beginning in *e* in the present and throughout the future and conditional. All verbs whose infinitive ends in -*oyer* or -*uyer* undergo this change. Verbs in -*ayer* may change the *y* to *i* or keep the spelling with *y*. Both spellings are in use for the verbs in -*ayer*. See the example below.

INFINITIVE	PRESENT	FUTURE
broyer (to crush, grind)	il broie	il broiera
appuyer (to press, support)	il appuie	il appuiera
payer (to pay)	il paie, il paye	il paiera, il payera

SAMPLE SENTENCES

1. Née dans les laboratoires de recherches, elle (i.e., la radio-cristallographie) *ne tarda pas à* s'en sortir pour pénétrer dans les établissements industriels.

2. Nous avons également réalisé des décharges sur des cellules constituées *à partir* d'autres bioxydes actifs.

3. Tout d'abord il *vaut la peine* de noter que l'ouvrier peut acheter deux fois plus de produits que le même ouvrier *il y a* 30 ans ne pouvait le faire.

4. La conférence avait pour but de *mettre sur pied* un modus vivendi.

5. Nous avons dit, *tout à l'heure,* qu'il est extrêmement probable que la courbe ait une allure régulière.

6. *La mise en route* a été effectuée en 1946.

7. *En fin de compte,* les balances annuelles ne comporteront plus que des écarts très faibles.

8. Dans chacun des demi-plans, situés *de part et d'autre* de cette droite, $J_{(x)}$ représentera évidemment une fonction continue.

9. L'expérience *a beau dire:* "c'est faux" et le raisonnement: "c'est absurde."

10. *Il y a longtemps que* l'on s'est aperçu que le soleil nous porte à la joie et à la gaîté.

11. Tous les pigments sombres *viennent s'accumuler* au centre des chromatophores.

EXERCISE

Dans cet article, on développe l'étude des corpuscules élémentaires et l'on montre les conclusions qu'on peut en tirer quant à la détermination de la constitution des atomes.

On envisage successivement la notion de masse et celle de spin, la fonction associée à un corpuscule et l'équation d'onde correspondante. On montre ensuite comment il est possible de proposer un mécanisme concret relatif aux interactions électriques qui permet d'éliminer la notion intrinsèque d'électricité et de ramener ainsi tous les phénomènes connus aux seules formes à priori de la sensibilité et de l'entendement.

L'atome est ensuite étudié de façon assez détaillée. On passe en revue les grandeurs quantifiées qui caractérisent ses négatons, puis on s'attache à la détermination des zones de localisation de chaque catégorie d'électrons σ et d'électrons π qui sont devenues si essentielles en chimie organique par exemple.

Enfin, on montre comment ces notions s'appliquent avec fécondité à l'étude de la structure électronique des éléments en liaison avec la classification périodique, dans le but de préparer un prochain article qui sera surtout destiné à l'exposition des règles du calcul des valences.

Le mouvement, tel est le seul concept qui demeure aujourd'hui nécessaire à la reconstitution du Monde avec les données de la raison.

La matière, l'électricité, qui nous semblaient des entités indispensables, peuvent être envisagées comme des formes particulières du mouvement.

Un corpuscule élémentaire se ramène à un simple tourbillon d'éther: pur mouvement dans l'espace le plus vide. Si merveilleux que puisse paraître ce résultat, il pouvait être prévu par une analyse philosophique suffisamment précise.—R. DAUDEL, "Les Agrégats atomiques," *Mouvement Scientifique,* No. 3225, Paris, Oct. 1943, p. 397.

The Subjunctive

The forms of the various verbs in the subjunctive have been described earlier, Table 5 for irregular verbs, Table 6 and Table 7 for regular verbs and endings. The matter of the uses of the subjunctive tenses has been left until last because most of these cause no trouble. It is almost true to say that the translator does not need to take into account when or why or how the subjunctive is used. If he knows the verb from which the particular form comes and its tense, he can translate as though he were dealing with an indicative.

Pour qu'elle soit valable . . .—In order that it may be valid . . .

Il faut qu'on se garde de la troubler.—One must guard against agitating it. (Take care not to agitate it.)

Comme s'il se fût agi d'autre chose . . .—As though it were (or "had been") a question of something else . . .

The examples show how the English frequently uses a subjunctive in cases similar to the French. Certain expressions in both languages require a subjunctive verb in the clause which they introduce. "In order to" and "for fear that," for instance. We

cannot say "In order that he is here on time." We must say "In
order that he be (may be, or should be) here on time." In French
the list of such expressions is much longer. Moreover, not only
subordinate conjunctions but also several verbs and verbal expressions require the Frenchman to use a subjunctive after them.

Following is a partial list of French subordinate conjunctions
which require the subjunctive in the following subordinate clause:

afin que—in order that	avant que—before
pour que—in order that	sans que—without
bien que—although	jusqu'à ce que—until
quoi que—although	autant que—as far as
pourvu que—provided that	quoi que—whatever
à moins que—unless	qui que—whoever

Verbs which require the subjunctive in a following subordinate
clause express an immediate personal interest or emotion on the
part of the subject. Verbs of wishing, doubting, fearing, regret-
ting, for instance:

Il veut que ce soit la fin—He wants it to be the end.
Il doute que ce soit la fin—He doubts that it is the end.
Il craint que ce ne* soit la fin—He fears that it is the end.
Il regrette que ce soit la fin—He regrets that it is the end.

Certain verbal expressions for "one must, it is necessary, it is
possible, it is better, it seems" require the subjunctive:

Il faut qu'on fasse attention—We (one) must watch out (pay attention).

Il se peut qu'elle finisse de bouillir—It is possible that it will stop
boiling, it may stop boiling.

---

* Note the extra *ne* which is quite often present in such subordinate
clauses with the subjunctive. It has no value and cannot be translated. (See
other examples of this meaningless *ne* on pp. 66–67.) If the author wished to
make the *soit* negative, he would put *pas* after it. Only with *cesser, oser,
pouvoir,* and *savoir,* does *ne* alone make the sense negative.

Il semble qu'il y ait quelque méprise—There seems to be some misunderstanding.

All the above examples show the subjunctive where it adds nothing to the information of the reader. Just as we are usually unaware when we are using the subjunctive in English, so are the French when they use it. Mainly the subjunctive is called forth automatically by the construction, a matter of conforming to the rules governing the code which is our language.

The subjunctive in French really has a special meaning in a few cases. If the speaker wants to express his doubt or uncertainty, his unwillingness to vouch for a fact, he may do so in a few types of descriptive clauses by using the subjunctive, whereas the indicative in the same construction would be more affirmative.

Je cherche une règle qui n'a pas d'exceptions—I am looking for a rule which has no exceptions. (Implies that such rules exist.)

Je cherche une règle qui n'ait pas d'exceptions—I am looking for a rule which has no exceptions. (The speaker would like such a rule but is not willing to commit himself as to its existence.)

C'est la meilleure solution que nous avons vue—It (That) is the best solution we have seen. (Simple statement of fact.)

C'est la meilleure solution que nous ayons vue—It (That) is the best solution we have seen. (Implies that there may well be a better one.)

Another use of the subjunctive, quite uncommon in technical work, except for *soit*, is the imperative use.

Soit x = 5—Let x = 5.

Qu'il en finisse—Let him get it over with.

Qu'ils reviennent plus tard—Have them (Let them) come back later.

Only the present subjunctive is used in this way and it is one of two cases where the subjunctive is found in the main clause of a sentence, the other being in instances where the imperfect (*eût*) or pluperfect subjunctive (*eût été*) substitutes for the conditional (would) or conditional perfect (would have). See sample sentences 14, 15, and 16 below.

TENSES OF THE SUBJUNCTIVE

Tradition has laid down rules about the time relationship which the various subjunctive tenses express with respect to the verb of the main part of the sentence.

Present Subjunctive

The present subjunctive indicates the same time as the main verb of the sentence.

Il *faut* qu'on se *rende* compte—One must realize
Il *faudra* qu'on se *rende* compte—One must realize (future)
Il *fallait* qu'on se *rende* compte—It was necessary to realize

Imperfect Subjunctive

The imperfect subjunctive is gradually being replaced by the present subjunctive. Formerly it was used instead of the present subjunctive to show the same time as that of the main verb whenever the latter was in one of the past tenses. It is still used occasionally in technical writing but is more and more confined to formal style.

Il *fallait* qu'on se *rendît* compte—It was necessary to realize
Il *fallut* qu'on se *rendît* compte—It was necessary to realize

Perfect Subjunctive

The perfect subjunctive (formed with the present subjunctive of the auxiliary plus the past participle) shows time previous to that of the main verb.

Il *faut* qu'on se *soit rendu* compte—One must have realized

Il *faudra* qu'on se *soit rendu* compte—It will be necessary to have realized

Il *fallait* qu'on se *soit rendu* compte—It was necessary to have realized

Pluperfect Subjunctive

Like the imperfect subjunctive, the pluperfect subjunctive (formed of the imperfect subjunctive of the auxiliary plus the past participle) is dying out in French. It is being replaced by the perfect but is still used in formal writing.

Il *fallait* qu'on se *fût rendu* compte—It was necessary to have realized

Il *fallut* qu'on se *fût rendu* compte—It was necessary to have realized

Summary of Uses of the Subjunctive

In a few cases the subjunctive will be used to interject a personal bias into a statement, and in a few others it serves to give an order. Otherwise it rarely needs to be considered by the translator as any different from the indicative.

SAMPLE SENTENCES

1. Supposons maintenant que la relation (5) étant satisfaite, le nombre *n soit* pair.

2. Il est important de souligner que, bien que les cas où interviennent des discontinuités *soient* les plus frappants, l'étude des phénomènes d'onde n'a pas été posée sous cette forme.

3. Supposons de plus, qu'à l'instant quelconque *t*, il n'y *ait* en vibration qu'une certaine couche d'air.

4. Tous les Etats ont voté de telles lois qui visent à assurer le paiement par le patron d'indemnités à son employé à la suite d'un accident quel que *soit* le responsable de cet accident.

5. Quelque grand que *soit* α et quelque petit que *soit* β, on aura l'equation suivante.

6. La fonction $f_{(x)}$ reste holomorphe de quelque manière qu'on *fasse* varier le point *x*, à condition qu'il ne *vienne* se confondre avec un point situé sur le segment.

7. Le radar parce qu'il «voit», quelles que *soient* les conditions de visibilité humaine, fournit près des côtes les connaissances nécessaires au pilotage.

8. *Soit,* par exemple, à représenter graphiquement le tableau précédent.

9. Je crains que les discussions à ce sujet ne *soient* pas abordées avec une objectivité suffisante.

10. On comprend assez aisément que, quand un électron évolue dans le domaine limité que constitue l'atome, son onde associée *puisse* être susceptible de prendre des formes stationnaires.

11. Notre dignité nous demandait de ne pas attendre que l'on nous *rappelât* à l'ordre.

12. Il n'est donc pas interdit d'espérer que celle-ci *puisse* réviser sa doctrine sur ce point.

13. Que *D* *soit* constant ou dépende de la concentration, on peut chercher *D* comme fonction de *u*.

14. J'aurais souhaité enfin que *fût* clairement posé le problème monétaire international.

15. Il *eût été* étonnant qu'on n'*eût* jamais *soupçonné* une division aussi nette, aussi régulière.

16. Cela *eût* entraîné une infinitésimale et momentanée dépréciation du franc par rapport au dollar.

17. Qu'on *veuille* l'avouer ou non, que la morale le réprouve ou pas, le cours "libre" se rapprochait bien plus de la réalité.

18. Il semble qu'il *faille* retourner la proposition.

19. Ils savent aussi que le Congrès des Etats-Unis ne concevait pas qu'il lui *fût* possible d'alimenter une Europe ne faisant rien pour s'aider elle-même.

20. Le catalyseur n'est pas modifié chimiquement bien que sa structure physique *puisse* être considérablement changée.

Conjugation of Avoir and Etre

Note: The translations given are not the only possible ones. The reader should consult the chapters on verbs and the appendix on the subjunctive for additional possibilities.

AVOIR

Tenses	*j'* or *je*—I	*il*—he, it *elle*[1]—she, it
Present	ai—have	a—has
Compound past	ai eu—had	a eu—had
Imperative		ait—may he[1] (let him[1]) have
Imperfect	avais—had	avait—had
Pluperfect	avais eu—had had	avait eu—had had
Future	aurai—will have	aura—will have
Future perfect	aurai eu—will have had	aura eu—will have had
Conditional	aurais—would have	aurait—would have
Cond. perfect	aurais eu—would have had	aurait eu—would have had
Past definite	eus—had	eut—had
Past anterior	eus eu—had had	eut eu—had had
Present subjunctive	aie—have	ait—have
Perfect subjunctive	aie eu—have had	ait eu—have had
Imperfect subjunctive	eusse—had	eût—had
Pluperfect subjunctive	eusse eu—had had	eût eu—had had

Infinitive *avoir*—to have
Perfect infinitive *avoir eu*—to have had

---

[1] Or any other third person singular subject, noun or pronoun.

AVOIR (continued)

nous—we	*vous*—you	*ils*—they *elles*[2]—they
avons—have	avez—have	ont—have
avons eu—had	avez eu—had	ont eu—had
ayons—let us have	ayez—have!	aient—let them[2] (may they[2]) have
avions—had	aviez—had	avaient—had
avions eu—had had	aviez eu—had had	avaient eu—had had
aurons—will have	aurez—will have	auront—will have
aurons eu—will have had	aurez eu—will have had	auront eu—will have had
aurions—would have	auriez—would have	auraient—would have
aurions eu—would have had	auriez eu—would have had	auraient eu—would have had
eûmes—had	eûtes—had	eurent—had
eûmes eu—had had	eûtes eu—had had	eurent eu—had had
ayons—have	ayez—have	aient—have
ayons eu—have had	ayez eu—have had	aient eu—have had
eussions—had	eussiez—had	eussent—had
eussions eu—had had	eussiez eu—had had	eussent eu—had had

Present participle *ayant*—having
Past participle *eu*[3]—had
Perfect participle *ayant eu*—having had

---

[2] Or any other third person plural subject, noun or pronoun.

[3] *eu* may add *-e* for feminine, and *-s* for plural to agree with nouns or pronouns referred to. Example: . . . *les solutions que nous avons eues* = . . . the solutions (which) we had.

ETRE

Tenses	*j'* or *je*—I	*il*—he, it *elle*[1]—she, it
Present	suis—am	est—is
Compound past	ai été—had	a été—was
Imperative		soit—may he[1] (let him[1]) be
Imperfect	étais—was	était—was
Pluperfect	avais été—had been	avait été—had been
Future	serai—will be	sera—will be
Future perfect	aurai été—will have been	aura été—will have been
Conditional	serais—would be	serait—would be
Cond. perfect	aurais été—would have been	aurait été—would have been
Past definite	fus—was	fut—was
Past anterior	eus été—had been	eut été—had been
Present subjunctive	sois—am, be	soit—is, be
Perfect subjunctive	aie été—have been	ait été—has been
Imperfect subjunctive	fusse—were, be	fût—were, be
Pluperfect subjunctive	eusse été—had been	eût été—had been

Infinitive *être*—to be
Perfect infinitive *avoir été*—to have been

---

[1] Or any other third person singular subject, noun or pronoun.

ETRE (continued)

nous—we	vous—you	ils—they elles[2]—they
sommes—are	êtes—are	sont—are
avons été—were	avez été—were	ont été—were
soyons—let us be	soyez—be!	soient—let them[2] (may they[2]) be
étions—were	étiez—were	étaient—were
avions été—had been	aviez été—had been	avaient été—had been
serons—will be	serez—will be	seront—will be
aurons été—will have been	aurez été—will have been	auront été—will have been
serions—would be	seriez—would be	seraient—would be
aurions été—would have been	auriez été—would have been	auraient été—would have been
fûmes—were	fûtes—were	furent—were
eûmes été—had been	eûtes été—had been	eurent été—had been
soyons—are, be	soyez—are, be	soient—are, be
ayons été—have been	ayez été—have been	aient été—have been
fussions—were, be	fussiez—were, be	fussent—were, be
eussions été—had been	eussiez été—had been	eussent été—had been

Present participle *étant*—being
Past participle *été*—been
Perfect participle *ayant été*—having been

---

[2] Or any other third person plural subject, noun or pronoun.

Alphabetical List
of Irregular Verb Forms

(Abbreviations: *def.*, definite; *fut.*, future; *imperf.*, imperfect; *indic.*, indicative; *part.*, participle; *pers.*, person; *pres.*, present; *pl.*, plural; *sing.*, singular; *subj.*, subjunctive.)

Accroissant, *pres. part.* **accroître,** to increase, augment

Accru, *past part.* **accroître,** to increase, augment

Acquerra, *fut.* **acquérir,** to acquire

Acquiert, *pres. indic.* **acquérir,** to acquire

Acquis, *past part.* **acquérir,** to acquire

Aille, *pres. subj.* **aller,** to go

Ait, *pres. subj.* **avoir,** to have

Asseyant (s'), *pres. part.* (s') **asseoir,** to sit down

Asseyera (s'), *fut.* (s') **asseoir,** to sit down

Assiéra (s'), *fut.* (s') **asseoir,** to sit down

Assied (s'), *pres. indic.* (s') **asseoir,** to sit down

Assis, *past part.* (s')**asseoir,** to sit down

Assoit (s'), *pres. indic.* (s') **asseoir,** to sit down

Assoira (s'), *fut.* (s')**asseoir,** to sit down

Assoyant (s'), *pres. part.* (s') **asseoir,** to sit down

Aura, *fut.* **avoir,** to have

Avançant, *pres. part.* **avancer,** to advance

Ayant, *pres. part.* **avoir,** to have

Boive, *pres. subj.* **boire,** to drink

Bu, *past part.* **boire,** to drink

Buvant, *pres. part.* **boire,** to drink

Clos, *past part.* **clore,** to close, enclose

Conduit, *pres., past def., past part.* **conduire,** to drive

Confisant, *pres. part.* **confire,** to pickle

Confit, *past part.* **confire,** to pickle

Connaissant, *pres. part.* **connaître,** to know

Connu, *past part.* **connaître,** to know

Cousant, *pres. part.* **coudre,** to sew

Cousu, *past part.* **coudre,** to sew

Couvert, *past part.* **couvrir,** to cover

Craignant, *pres. part.* **craindre,** to fear

Craint, *past part.* **craindre,** to fear

Croissant, *pres. part.* **croître,** to grow

Croit, *pres.* **croire,** to believe

Croît, *pres.* **croître,** to grow

Croyant, *pres. part.* **croire,** to believe

Cru, *past part.* **croire,** to believe

Crû, *past part.* **croître,** to grow

Cuisant, *pres. part.* **cuire,** to cook

Déchu, *past part.* **déchoir,** to go to ruin

Devant, *pres. part.* **devoir,** to be to, to have to, etc.

Disant, *pres. part.* **dire,** to say

Dit, *past part.* **dire,** to say

Doit, *pres. indic.* **devoir,** to owe

Dut, *past def.* **devoir,** to owe

Dû, *past part.* **devoir,** to owe

Echéant, *pres. part.* **échoir,** to fall due

Echu, *past part.* **échoir,** to fall due

Ecrivant, *pres. part.* **écrire,** to write

Enverra, *fut.* **envoyer,** to send

Envoie, *pres. indic.* **envoyer,** to send

Est, *pres. indic.* **être,** to be

Eté, *past part.* **être,** to be

Etes, *pres. indic.* **être,** to be

Eu, *past part.* **avoir,** to have

Eut, *past def.* **avoir,** to have

Eût, *imperf. subj.* **avoir,** to have

Faille, *pres. subj.* **falloir,** to be necessary

Faisant, *pres. part.* **faire,** to make, do

Fait, *past part.* **faire,** to make, do

Fallu, *past part.* **falloir,** to be necessary

Fasse, *pres. subj.* **faire,** to make, do

Faudra, *fut.* **falloir,** to be necessary

Faut, *pres. indic.* **falloir,** to be necessary

Fera, *fut.* **faire,** to make, do

Fit, *past def.* **faire,** to make, do

Font, *pres. indic.* (3rd pers. pl.) **faire,** to make, do

Fut, *past def.* **être,** to be

Fût, *imperf. subj.* **être,** to be

Fuyant, *pres. part.* **fuir,** to flee, leak

Ira, *fut.* **aller,** to go

Joignant, *pres. part.* **joindre,** to join

Joint, *past part.* **joindre,** to join

Lisant, *pres. part.* **lire,** to read

Lu, *past part.* **lire,** to read

Lut, *past def.* **lire,** to read

Lui, *past part.* **luire,** to shine

Luisant, *pres. part.* **luire,** to shine

Mangeant, *pres. part.* **manger,** to eat

Mène, *pres. indic.* **mener,** to lead

Mènera, *fut.* **mener,** to lead

Mettra, *fut.* **mettre,** to put

Meut (se), *pres. indic.* (se) **mouvoir,** to move

Meurt, *pres. indic.* **mourir,** to die

Mis *past part.* **mettre,** to put, place

Mit, *past def.* **mettre,** to put, place

Mort, *past part.* **mourir,** to die

Moulant, *pres. part.* **moudre,** to grind

Moulu, *past part.* **moudre,** to grind

Mû, *past part.* (se) **mouvoir,** to move

Mut (se), *past def.* (se) **mouvoir,** to move

Naissant, *pres. part.* **naître,** to be born

Naquit, *past def.* **naître,** to be born

Né, *past part.* **naître,** to be born

Nettoie, *pres.* **nettoyer,** to clean

Nui, *past part.* **nuire,** to hurt, harm

Nuisant, *pres. part.* **nuire,** to hurt, harm

Ouvert, *past part.* **ouvrir,** to open

Ont, *pres. indic.* **avoir,** to have

Paie, *pres. indic.* **payer,** to pay

Paye, *pres. indic.* **payer,** to pay

Paru, *past part.* **paraître,** to appear

Peignant, *pres. part.* **peindre,** to paint

Peint, *past part.* **peindre,** to paint

Peut, *pres. indic.* **pouvoir,** can, to be able

Plaisant, *pres. part.* **plaire,** to please

Pleut, *pres. indic.* **pleuvoir,** to rain (down)

Plu, *past part.* **pleuvoir,** to rain (down)

Plu, *past part.* **plaire,** to please

Plut, *past def.* **pleuvoir,** to rain (down)

Plut, *past def.* **plaire,** to please

Pourra, *fut.* **pouvoir,** can, to be able

Pourvoyant, *pres. part.* **pourvoir,** to provide

Pourvu, *past part.* **pourvoir,** to provide

Prenant, *pres. part.* **prendre,** to take

Pris, *past part.* **prendre,** to take

Prit, *past def.* **prendre,** to take

Pu, *past part.* **pouvoir,** can, to be able

Put, *past def.* **pouvoir,** can, to be able

Puisse, *pres. subj.* **pouvoir,** can, to be able

Reçu, *past part.* **recevoir,** to receive

Repu, *pres. part.* **repaître,** to feed (**repu,** satiated)

Résolu, *past part.* **résoudre,** to resolve

Résolvant, *pres. part.* **résoudre,** to resolve

Résous, *past part.* **résoudre,** to resolve

Résoute, *fem. past part.* **résoudre,** to resolve

Ri, *past part.* **rire,** to laugh

Riant, *pres. part.* **rire,** to laugh

Sachant, *pres. part.* **savoir,** to know

Sait, *pres. indic.* **savoir,** to know

Saura, *fut.* **savoir,** to know

Sera, *fut.* **être,** to be

Soient, *pres. subj.* **être,** to be

Soit, *pres. subj.* **être,** to be

Sommes, *pres. indic.* **être,** to be

Sont, *pres. indic.* **être,** to be

Souffert, *past part.* **souffrir,** to suffer

Soustrait, *past part.* **soustraire,** to subtract

Soustrayant, *pres. part.* **soustraire,** to subtract

Su, *past part.* **savoir,** to know

Suis, *pres. indic.* **être,** to be; *pres. indic.* **suivre,** to follow

Sut, *past def.* **savoir,** to know

Suffisant, *pres. part.* **suffire,** to suffice

Sursis, *past part.* **surseoir,** to postpone

Sursoyant, *pres. part.* **surseoir,** to postpone

Taisant, *pres. part.* **taire,** to keep silent

Tenu, *past part.* **tenir,** to hold

Tiendra, *fut.* **tenir,** to hold

Tient, *pres. indic.* (*sing.*) **tenir,** to hold

Tienne, *pres. subj.* **tenir,** to hold

Tint, *past. def.* **tenir,** to hold

Trait, *past part.* **traire,** to milk

Trayant, *pres. part.* **traire,** to milk

Tu, *past part.* **taire,** to keep silent

Va, *pres. indic.* **aller,** to go

Vaille, *pres. subj.* **valoir,** to be worth

Vaincu, *past part.* **vaincre,** to conquer, win out

Vainquant, *pres. part.* **vaincre,** to conquer, win out

Valant, *pres. part.* **valoir,** to be worth

Valu, *past part.* **valoir,** to be worth

Vaut, *pres. indic.* (*sing.*) **valoir,** to be worth

Vécu, *past part.* **vivre,** to live

Verra, *fut.* **voir,** to see

Vêtu, *past part.* **vêtir,** to clothe

Veut, *pres. indic.* **vouloir,** to wish

Viendra, *fut.* **venir,** to come

Vienne, *pres. subj.* **venir,** to come

Vient, *pres. indic.* **venir,** to come

Vint, *past def.* **venir,** to come

Vit, *past def.* **voir,** to see; also *past def.* **vivre,** to live

Voit, *pres. indic.* (*3d pers. sing.*) **voir,** to see

Vont, *pres. indic.* (*3d pers. pl.*) **aller,** to go

Voudra, *fut.* **vouloir,** to wish

Voulu, *past part.* **vouloir,** to wish

Voyant, *pres. part.* **voir,** to see

Vu, *past part.* **voir,** to see